TRADE UNIONS
IN EUROPE

TRADE UNIONS
IN EUROPE

Margaret Stewart

Employment Conditions Abroad Ltd/Gower Economic Publications

First published in Great Britain by Gower Press Limited, Epping, Essex
1974

ISBN 0 7161 0216 1

Gower Economic Publications is the subsidiary imprint of Gower Press specializing in the
research and publication of economic reviews and location studies. Each review is
regularly updated allowing for the inclusion of the latest statistical data and comments.

Set in 11/13 Press Roman and printed in Great Britain by
Eyre & Spottiswoode Ltd at Grosvenor Press

Contents

Illustrations

Maps

Maps showing population densities in the principal regions of:

Preface

Information is essential to understanding and understanding is essential to good industrial relations. This survey of trade unions in the European Economic Community has been written in the hope and belief that the information it contains will help towards better understanding, and thereby help to promote better industrial relations.

There are wide variations between the industrial relations and collective bargaining systems of the different countries, and between the strength and structures of the various trade unions. But, whatever methods are employed, all unions have in common a basic purpose, which is to advance the interests and influence of their members.

In nearly all the countries surveyed, unions are demanding greater status and recognition and a greater voice in the counsels of industry. They are no longer content to be passive and 'sleeping' partners and their aspirations cannot be ignored by industry or governments.

Within the EEC itself, trade unions are coming to play an ever-increasing role and are pressing for a greater say in economic and social policy-making. They are associated with many of the Commission's institutions, as indeed are the employers' organizations. Their attitudes towards such issues as multinational corporations and codetermination are of crucial concern.

This book is in two parts; Part One gives background information. Chapter 1 compares the development of trade unions in the nine countries of the European Economic Community and the current state of their membership and organization. It looks at the wide differences in structure and methods, comparing the highly centralized German system with the fragmented character of the French unions and the pluralism of those in the Benelux countries. It highlights some of the salient features — what the unions have in common as well as how they differ.

Chapters 2 and 3 deal with the development of international union organizations, culminating in the foundation of the European Trade Union Confederation in the Spring of 1973. These chapters also describe the institutions of the European Community which have a bearing on labour and social matters and considers recent developments in the Community's social policies. Chapter 4 examines some of the major issues confronting European unions, such as workers' participation and multinational companies.

Part Two contains country-by-country surveys of the different unions in the Nine. There are obviously variations in treatment but the same broad pattern is adopted throughout.

Each chapter, preceded by a brief factual note about the country, sets out membership, structure, central organization, methods of collective bargaining, industrial relations and cooperation, with a brief assessment of some of the results of collective bargaining.

The subject is so vast that each survey of individual countries could be expanded into a separate book. For reasons of space and readability, it has been necessary to compress much of the information and present it in tabular form, where possible. Trade unions, however, do not easily lend themselves to tabulation. There are often discrepancies in figures and estimates of membership, for example, and it is difficult to get comparable up-to-date figures. Unions are concerned with human and social values, which cannot be measured statistically.

The information has been collected from official sources, from employers' and union organizations, and from published and unpublished material. Much of it is derived from personal interviews and visits during 1972 and 1973 to France, Germany, Belgium, Italy, Luxembourg, the Netherlands, Ireland and Geneva, as well as from innumerable London sources.

This is a book about trade unions, so the bulk of the information has been derived from union sources. I have sought to be factual and objective, and to avoid the expression of personal opinions.

Appendices contain a list of sources and a bibliography, and a selection of useful addresses. There is a guide to help the reader through the tangle of initials which characterizes all national and international organizations.

The political, monetary and agricultural aspects of the Community have not been dealt with and I have only touched in passing on social security and benefits. This book was written before the energy and economic crises of winter 1973/74 which have clearly had massive effects on economic and social developments within the EEC. This situation, however, in no way affects the information contained in the book about the long-term objectives of trade unions.

A Note about
Employment Conditions Abroad Limited

Employment Conditions Abroad Limited is an organization established by a number of major international companies who are represented in some 167 countries and who felt the need for a central clearing-house of information. Its object is to collect, analyse and distribute up-to-date comprehensive and factual reports, linked with an enquiry service, about terms and conditions of employment throughout the world covering both expatriate and national employees.

The information includes such aspects as remuneration comparisons, allowances and fringe benefits, personal income tax, living costs and conditions and education resources for children. Many other aspects, such as employment legislation, work permits and procedures, and tax treatment of expatriate remuneration are covered in addition to the related background of the general political, financial, economic and industrial relations situation in each country.

For nearly three years the organization has steadily built up this data bank of information based on the network of communications provided from its own member companies and collected from many other authoritative sources. Cost-of-living surveys have been carried out in 50 countries and have formed the base of an independent weighted price index for the use of members. The number of countries covered will increase year by year.

The information services are designed specifically for the use of companies that have interests in countries outside their own home base, and is on a membership basis.

Full details can be obtained by contacting:

> J. H. G. Firth
> Executive Director
> Employment Conditions Abroad Limited
> 9 Orme Court
> London W2 4RL
> Telephone: 01–229 3262

Acknowledgements

A lot of people have given me help and advice, but the responsibility for the book is my own.

I would particularly like to thank the following for their help:

At the Commission's Brussels headquarters:
Mr Michael Shanks
Mr Jack Peel
Mr Gianfranco Giro
Members of the press and information division.

The following have been helpful with suggestions and have been kind enough to read the relevant chapter:
Mr H. A. L. Bulpitt, Labour Attaché, Paris
Mr Cyril Marshall, Labour Attaché, Brussels
Dr R. Vollmer, Labour Attaché at the German Embassy, London
Mr Donal Niven, assistant general secretary, Irish TUC
Dr S. Ferrari, International Centre, Institute for Advanced Technical and Vocational Training, Turin

Representatives of the Fiat management and Dr Di Mattino, Generale, Milan.
Mr Erik Ohrt, Danish Management Centre, Copenhagen
Mr A. Tarp, Employers Federation
International Department of the Landsorganisationen i Danmark
Mr A. F. Rice, Federated Union of Employers, Dublin
Officials of the Labour Court, Dublin
Representatives of the Fédération générale du travail de Belgique and the Christian trade unions in Brussels.

Representatives of the Confédération générale du travail and other union centres in Paris
Mr T. Barry-Braunthal, International Confederation of Free Trade Unions, Brussels and other officers

In Geneva, I had great help from officers of the International Metalworkers Federation and the International Union of Food and Allied Workers. Unfortunately Mr C. Levinson, International Federation of Chemical and General Workers Unions withheld cooperation, so I have not referred to the ICF activities.

For UK I received assistance from:
International Labour Office (London), especially Mrs G. Sampson, librarian
Officials of the TUC
The Information Office, EEC, London
The Amalgamated Union of Engineering Workers
Many other individuals and organizations provided assistance.

Thanks are due to Miss Ena Mitchell for help with the Italian translations and to Miss Sofka Knight for secretarial assistance.

List of Abbreviations

International and European

ECSC	European Coal and Steel Community
EEC	European Economic Community
EFTA	European Free Trade Association
EMF	European Metalworkers Federation
EO–WCL	European Organization–World Confederation of Labour
ETUC	European Trade Union Confederation
FIET	International Federation of Commercial, Clerical and Technical Employees
ICF	International Federation of Chemical and General Workers Unions
ICFTU	International Confederation of Free Trade Unions
ILO	International Labour Organization
IMF	International Metalworkers Federation
IOE	International Organization of Employers
ITS	International Trade Secretariats
IUF	International Union of Food and Allied Workers' Association
OECD	Organization for Economic Cooperation and Development
UNICE	Union des industries de la communauté européenne
WCL	World Confederation of Labour
WFTU	World Federation of Trade Unions

Belgium

CGSLB   Centre général des syndicats libéraux (Federation of Liberal Unions)
CSC   Confédération des syndicats chrétiens (Confederation of Christian Trade Unions)
FBE   Fédération des entreprises de Belgique (Federation of Belgian Enterprises)
FGTB   Fédération générale de travail de Belgique (Belgian Federation of Labour)

Denmark

DA   Dansk Arbejdsgiverforening (Danish Employers' Confederation)
LO   Landsorganisationen i Danmark (Federation of Danish Trade Unions)

France

CFDT   Confédération française démocratique du travail
CGT   Confédération générale du travail
CGT–FO   Confédération générale du travail–Force ouvrière
CNPF   Conseil national du patronat français

Federal Republic of Germany

BDA   Bundesvereinigung des Deutschen Arbeitgeberverbände (Confederation of Employers' Associations)
DGB   Deutsche Gewerkschaftsbund (Trades Union Confederation)

Ireland

FUE   Federated Union of Employers
ICTU   Irish Congress of Trade Unions
ITGWU   Irish Transport and General Workers' Union

Italy

ACLI	Christian Association of Italian Workers
CGIL	Confederazione generale italiana del lavoro (Italian General Confederation of Labour)
CISL	Confederazione italiana del sindacati lavoratori (Italian Confederation of Christian Unions)
UIL	Unione italiana del lavoro (Italian Union of Labour)

Luxembourg

CGT	Confédération générale du travail
CLSC	Confédération luxembourgoise des syndicats chrétiens

Netherlands

CNV	Christelijk Nationaal Vakverbond (National Federation of Christian Trade Unions)
NCW	Nederlands Christelijk Werkgeversverbond
NKV	Nederlands Katholiek Vakverbond (Netherlands Federation of Catholic Trade Unions)
NVV	Nederlands Verbond van Vakverenigingen (Netherlands Federation of Trade Unions)
VNO	Verbond van Neederlandsche Ondernemingen

United Kingdom

AUEW	Amalgamated Union of Engineering Workers
CBI	Confederation of British Industry
GMWU	General and Municipal Workers Union
TGWU	Transport and General Workers Union
TUC	Trades Union Congress

PART ONE

THE EUROPEAN BACKGROUND

1

The European
Trade Union Pattern

A trade union was defined by Sidney and Beatrice Webb as 'a continuous association of wage-earners for the purpose of maintaining or improving the condition of their working lives'. This is still accepted as the classic definition of the purpose and objectives of democratic trade unions, and was quoted by the TUC in its evidence before the Royal Commission on Trade Unions in 1966. The constitutions of some European unions contain references to the 'overthrow of capitalism' or 'the establishment of a classless society' as their ultimate aims. But whatever their philosophies, all unions in practice regard their most important immediate function as being to bargain for better pay and conditions, in order to raise the living standards of the workers.

There are wide differences in the methods and strategies adopted by various European movements to attain their objectives, as there are in their organization and structure. The differences, however, lie in means rather than ends, and most are attributable to historical and traditional factors. This chapter seeks to identify some of the points that are common to the unions of Europe as well as differences between them. The situation in each EEC country is given in detail in Part Two.

Historical Development

European trade unions developed at different stages of the nineteenth century. Britain may be regarded as the founder of the movement, for the TUC held its inaugural conference in 1868, at a time when unions on the

Continent were still struggling for existence, if indeed they yet existed. For example, the French unions did not obtain the right to legal recognition until 1884 and did not form a central organization until 1895. Free association was banned in the Netherlands until 1872 and the first congress of the Italian chambers of labour was not held until 1893. In Germany, an anti-Socialist law, sponsored by Bismarck in 1878, effectively obstructed trade union, as well as political, development and only after it lapsed in the 1890s was the first effective central organization set up. Because many European unions were born in repression and had to operate in clandestine fashion, their early leaders tended to be more revolutionary in outlook than those in Britain. In Britain, in the heyday of the British Empire, many unions tended to look beyond Europe and several craft unions set up branches in Australia and America.

In the nineteenth century, the conflict between the Church and anti-clerical movements (which had been resolved in England in the sixteenth century) led to the division of many European unions on religious grounds and the establishment of 'confessional' unions. This was a disadvantage from which British unions have never suffered.

Much later, conflict arose between Socialists and Communists. This produced deep national and international schisms which were revived during the 'Cold War' period at the end of the Second World War. In France and Italy, Communist-led union centres continued to dominate the industrial scene. Elsewhere in Europe, the Communists exercised less influence.

The general result is that trade unions in the nine European Community countries present a patchwork picture, in regard to membership, organization and influence. There are altogether about 30 million trade unionists in the nine countries of the EEC, but there is no 'harmonization' of trade union patterns. The proportion of workers who belong to unions varies from country to country, as shown in Figure 1:1.

Figure 1:1   Degree of organization of workers

Year	Belgium	Germany	France	Italy	Luxembourg	Netherlands	UK	Ireland	Denmark (estimate)	TOTAL
1958	60	38	23	55-60	60	43	43	39	70	42
1969	67	37	22	55-60	55	41	46	48	70	42
1970	67	37	22	55-60	55	41	47	48	70	42
1971	67	37	22	55-60	55	41	not available	48	70	42

Source: *Social Situation in the Community 1972*, EEC, Brussels, 1973

National Characteristics

As well as history, religion and politics, differences in national characteristics and customs account for many of the existing divisions, and the variations in structure and membership.

The tradition of thoroughness and efficiency permeates German trade unions, as it does every other organization in the Federal Republic. German unions had the advantage of being completely reconstructed at the end of the Second World War (largely with help from the British TUC) and emerged with only 16 industrial unions and a powerful centralized TUC, without any ideological or sectarian barriers. In Britain, as in Germany, the movement is free from ideological differences and has only one national centre, the TUC. Structurally, however, the British movement (as shown in Chapter 13) is an amalgam of many organizations of differing types and sizes. Since the Irish movement was originally based on the British, there are strong structural resemblances between the two, with a centralized TUC and with no religious or sectarian barriers — but the Irish suffer from a multiplicity of unions. Denmark presents a combination of the German and British tendencies. Its unions are highly centralized with the LO (TUC) exerting an effective authority but their structure is based on occupational rather than industrial grouping.

In the five other countries of the EEC, the unions present a very different pattern. In France and Italy, they are still divided along political lines and the French have 5 different national centres. This is one of the reasons for their proportionately low membership. In both countries, there have been moves towards common action and in Italy these appear to be bearing fruit.

In the Benelux countries, the movement is likewise pluralistic, being basically divided between Socialist and Christian unions. Here, too, efforts to reach common agreement have been intensified. In Belgium, which has one of the most influential movements in Europe, the Socialists and the Christians, though opposed in philosophy, cooperate closely at national and local level. The same applies in the Netherlands. In both Belgium and the Netherlands, there has been a tendency for the Christian unions to broaden their base and to form alliances with the Socialists.

Social Conditions

Legislation in the Six countries covers such issues as the national minimum wage, hours, holidays, redundancy, training, works councils, as well as social security and industrial health and safety.

Social security, holidays and workers' protection are covered by legislation in the three new entrants to the Community, but there are no laws
relating to workers' participation. The position of workers in the Nine in
respect of holidays and hours is shown in Figures 1:2 and 1:3.

These tables show that there is much more similarity in working hours
than there is in respect of holidays. Although the length of the working week
varies, all EEC countries are moving towards the adoption of the 40-hour
week, in practice as well as in theory. The Italians enjoy the longest public
holidays and the British and Irish the shortest.

Standards of living vary from country to country according to national
tastes and habits, and it is therefore impossible to make meaningful
comparisons. All the Nine have been subject to inflation, as is shown in
Figure 1:4 which gives consumer prices and Figure 1:5 which gives earnings.

Collective Bargaining

Collective bargaining is the basic instrument by which all European unions
advance their aims. In the original Six countries, collective agreements are
frequently backed by legislation and the state often assumes a direct role in
industrial relations. Among the three new entrants, Britain, Ireland and
Denmark, there is more reliance on the voluntary system and in Britain,
before the Industrial Relations Act, industrial relations were less regulated
by law than in any other industrialized country.

Several tendencies common to all nine countries can be identified in the
field of collective bargaining. One is the continuing trend towards plant
bargaining, either to supplement industry-wide agreements or to negotiate
directly at company level. In the UK plant bargaining has been established
longer and is more highly developed than any other member country.

British unions were also the first in Europe to introduce the system of
workers' representation at factory level through shop stewards. Most Euro
pean movements now have parallel schemes, with representatives known as
'délégués syndicaux' in France and Belgium. The extent to which shop
stewards are officially recognized varies but most are protected against
dismissal and given time and facilities to carry out their union duties.

Another common trend is the inclusion of an ever-growing range of
subjects in the scope of collective bargaining. Fringe benefits, training,
redundancy, social security, work patterns and many issues as well as wages
and hours are the subject of negotiation. This move developed earlier in the
EEC six countries than in Britain.

Figure 1:2 Holidays

	Year	Belgium	Germany	France	Italy	Luxembourg	Netherlands	UK	Ireland	Denmark	TOTAL
Annual paid holidays (days) (Predominant systems)											
(a) Basic holidays for adults fixed by legislation	1958	12	12	18	—	8-18	—	—	12	12	—
	1969	18	15-18	24	—	18-24	10-12	—	12	18	—
	1970	18	15-18	24	—	18-24	10-12	—	12	18	—
	1971	18	15-18	24	12	18-24	12½-15	—	12	18	—
	1972	18	15-18	24	12	18-24	15-18	—	12	18	—
(b) Basic holidays for adults laid down in collective agreements	1958	12	12-18	18	12	8-18	12-15	12	12	18	8-18
	1969	18	16-24	24	12-14	18-24	15-16	12-18	12-18	18	12-24
	1970	18	16-24	24	12-15	18-24	15-18	12-18	18	18	12-24
	1971	18	16-24	24	13-18	18-24	15-19	12-18	18	18	12-24
	1972	20	17-24	24	13-18	18-24	16-20	—	—	21	12-24
Public holidays											
(a) Public holidays paid for and not worked fixed by legislation	1958	10	10-13	1	16	10	—	6	6	9½	—
	1969	10	10-13	1	16	10	—	6	6	9½	—
	1970	10	10-13	1	16	10	—	6	6	9½	—
	1971	10	10-13	1	16	10	—	6	6	9½	—
	1972	10	10-13	1	16	10	—	6	6	9½	—
(b) Public holidays paid for and not worked fixed by legislation and laid down in collective agreements	1958	10	10-13	4-7	17	10	7	6-7	6	9½	4-17
	1969	10	10-13	8-10	17	10	7	6-7	6	9½	6-17
	1970	10	10-13	8-10	17	10	7	6-7	6	9½	6-17
	1971	10	10-13	8-10	17	10	7	6-7	6	9½	6-17
	1972	10	10-13	8-10	17	10	7	6-7	6	9½	6-17

Source: *Social Situation in the Community*

Figure 1:3   Length of working week

Hours	Year	Belgium	Germany	France	Italy	Luxembourg (Employees/Workers)	Netherlands	UK	Ireland	Denmark	TOTAL
(a) Hours of work fixed by legislation	1958	48	48	40	48	44/48	48	—	48	—	40-48
	1969	45	48	40	48	44/48	48	—	48	—	40-48
	1970	45	48	40	48	44/48	48	—	48	—	40-48
	1971	45	48	40	48	44/44	48	—	48	—	40-48
	1972	45	48	40	48	40/44	48	—	48	—	40-48
(b) Hours of work fixed for manual workers in industry by collective agreements in general	1958	45-47	44-45	—	48	48	48	44-45	44	45-48	44-48
	1969	43-44	40-41½	—	42-44	42-44	43¾	40-41	42	42½	40-44
	1970	42-44	40-41	—	42-44	41-44	42½-43¾	40-41	41-42	42½-41¾	40-44
	1971	42-44	40-41	—	40-43	41-44	42½-43¾	40	40-42	41¾	40-44
	1972	41-42	40	—	40-42	40-44	41¼-42½	40	40-42	41¾	40-44

Source: *Social Situation in the Community*

Figure 1:4   Consumer prices (Index 1963 = 100)

	Belgium		Denmark		France		Germany		Ireland		Italy		Luxembourg		Netherlands		UK	
	General	Food	General	Food	General	Food	General	Food	General	Food	General	Food	General	Food	General	Food	General	Food
1964	104.2	104.9	103.5	102.4	103.4	103.6	102.4	102.2	106.7	106.2	105.9	104.9	103.1	101.8	106	106	103.3	102.9
1965	108.4	109.9	105.5	107	106.0	106.0	105.6	105.8	112.1	112.1	110.6	110.6	106.5	106.3	111	112	108.2	106.5
1966	112.9	115.3	112.9	113	108.9	108.9	109.5	109.1	115.4	113.4	113.2	112.8	110.1	103.9	117	118	112.5	110.3
1967	116.2	118.2	122.1	123	111.8	110.8	111.4	109.0	119.1	115.5	117.4	114.8	112.5	105.3	121.2	120.7	115.3	113.1
1968	119.4	120.2	131.9	134	116.9	114.2	113.1	108.1	124.7	122.2	119.0	115.1	115.4	109.2	125.7	123.7	120.7	117.6
1969	123.8	125.7	136.5	141	124.4	121.4	116.1	111.0	133.9	129.5	122.2	118.4	118.1	113.3	135.0	131.8	127.2	125.0
1970	128.7	130.1	145.4	153	130.9	128.5	121.4	114.2	145.0	139.4	128.2	123.5	123.5	119.1	141.0	137.5	135.3	133.7
1971	134.3	132.6	153.9	162	138.1	136.8	126.7	118.5	157.9	149.7	134.4	128.4	129.3	123.3	151.7	143.3	148.1	148.5
1972	141.6	141.4	164.0	177	146.2	146.0	134.0	125.8	171.6	167.4	172.1	136.5	136.1	131.6	163.5	152.7	158.6	161.6

Source: *ILO Bulletin of Labour Statistics*, first quarter 1973.

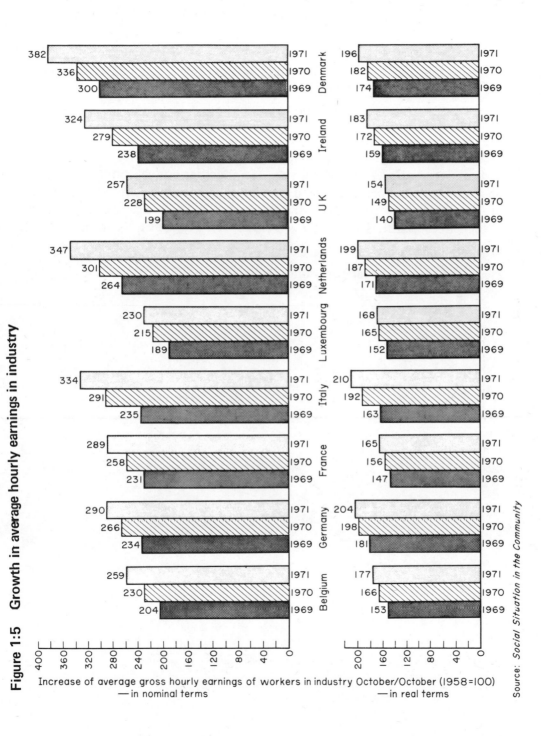

Figure 1:5   Growth in average hourly earnings in industry

Increase of average gross hourly earnings of workers in industry October/October (1958=100)
— in nominal terms   — in real terms

Source: *Social Situation in the Community*

Cooperation or Conflict?

As might be expected from their history and philosophies, unions differ widely in their attitudes towards cooperation, whether with employers or with government. In many European countries (not Britain or Ireland) works councils are backed by legislation. In some, for example, Germany, workers are represented on management supervisory boards (see page 108-9).

Similar arrangements are being planned in Belgium and Denmark and workers' representation is the subject of a draft Community directive (see Chapter 3).

The Germans are firm advocates of industrial cooperation in order to increase economic prosperity and provide their members with a bigger share of the national wealth. Relations between the DGB and the government headed by Socialist Herr Brandt are close. The French CGT and the Belgian Socialist FGTB are, broadly, against cooperating with capitalism and in

Figure 1:6   Index of labour productivity

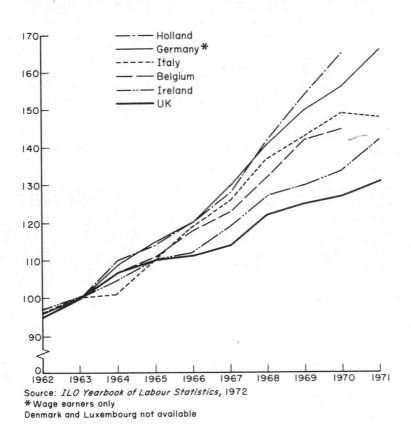

Source: *ILO Yearbook of Labour Statistics*, 1972
*Wage earners only
Denmark and Luxembourg not available

favour of direct workers' control. In Britain, most unions (though not the TUC as such) are linked with the Labour Party and advocate Socialist policies of public ownership. In Denmark, the unions work in partnership with the Socialist government, but believe in achieving Socialism through a fairer distribution of wealth rather than by nationalization.

The question, 'Conflict or cooperation?' is still a fundamental problem for unions to resolve but, in practice, trade union leaders in West Europe are realists. Even the militants are aware that they must work within the existing framework, if they are to win higher standards for their members.

The difference in national attitudes is reflected in statistics on improvements in productivity (Figure 1:6) and the number of days lost through industrial disputes (Figure 1:7). In Germany, a strike is a last resort, in Italy, it is the first. In some countries, for example, Germany and Denmark, legislation limits the right to strike during the currency of an agreement. In France and Italy, the right to strike is sacrosanct and is regarded as the main means of bringing pressure on employers and government.

Yet, throughout Europe at the beginning of the 1970s there were signs of increased militancy. In the Spring of 1973 a general strike took place in Denmark; there was a serious stoppage at Hoogovens steel plant in the Netherlands and a wave of strikes by engineering workers in Germany in August 1973 — all in countries with hitherto relatively strike-free records. Another new development has been the 'work-in' which supports the right to work by employees threatened by a factory closure. The Upper Clyde Shipyard workers were the first to adopt this tactic, which was taken up elsewhere in Britain. The most recent example in Europe was the occupation by the workers of the French watchmaking factory, Lip, at Besançon in the summer of 1973.

Figure 1:7 Days lost per thousand persons employed in mining, manufacturing, construction and transport

	1969	1970	1971	1972[1]
Belgium	100	840	720	180
Denmark[2]	80	170	30	40
France	200	280	3 320	530
Germany	20	10	340	—[3]
Ireland	2 170	490	660	590
Italy	4 160	1 730	1 060	1 680
Netherlands	10	140	50	70
UK	520	2 210	1 610	870

Source: ILO
[1] Preliminary figures
[2] Manufacturing only
[3] Less than five days lost per 1 000 persons employed

2

European Institutions

EEC Social and Employment Policy

The preamble to the Treaty of Rome (1957) laid down the general aim of the members of the European Economic Community as being 'the constant improvement of the living and working conditions of their peoples'. Member states agreed (article 117) on the need 'to promote improved working conditions and an improved standard of living for workers, so as to make possible their harmonization while the improvement is being maintained'. The Treaty, however, did not spell out the measures by which such 'harmonization' and 'improvement' could be achieved, though it required the Commission to promote 'close cooperation between member states in the social field', on such matters as employment, labour law, working conditions, training, social security, industrial health and safety, trade union law and collective bargaining.

The Treaty imposed specific obligations in only two main employment respects — free movement of labour (articles 48-51) and equal pay (article 119). The first called for the abolition of discrimination between Community nationals in employment, pay or working conditions. This article effectively came into force in 1968. In respect of 'the principle that men and women should receive equal pay for equal work', progress has been less rapid.

Figure 4:4 (page 42) shows the extent of the gap in different European countries.

Two other articles in the Treaty were concerned with employment conditions — one (article 80) urging the inter-Community exchange of young workers and another (article 118) calling for 'close cooperation' in the field of 'basic and advanced vocational training'.

Apart from this the carrying out of the Treaty's social objectives was left to individual nations and until recently the Commission paid relatively little attention to social problems, compared with the attention given to agriculture and trade problems. As Mr Michael Shanks has said 'The truth is that the *laissez-faire* orientation of the original Rome Treaty condemned social policy to a backwater for too long; and as a result not only the quality of Europe's life, but the cohesion of Europe's society and the efficiency of Europe's industries have suffered'. The Commission itself, in a report *'The development of the social situation in the Community'* (February 1973) noted: 'Up to now social policy has been very largely the uncoordinated sum total of the various reactions of the social body to the results and consequences of other policies'. But, it went on: 'This is now no longer the case. It is now accepted that social policy should be accepted in its own right', while Mr Shanks wrote: 'Social policy has been accorded the importance it deserves'

This change did not come as a result of some Pauline conversion of the heads of government. It had been discussed for some years in the lobbies and committee rooms of the EEC headquarters at Brussels and in the various capitals. But it was only in Paris in October 1972, at the summit meeting of heads of state that the new priority for social purposes was clearly and categorically stated. In the words of a post-summit declaration:

> Economic expansion is not an end in itself. Its first aim should be to enable disparities in living conditions to be reduced. It must take place with the participation of all the social partners. It should result in an improvement in the quality of life, as well as in standards of living.

According to the official communiqué, the

> Heads of state or government emphasized that they attached as much importance to vigorous action in the social field as to the achievement of economic and monetary union [and] thought it essential to ensure the increasing involvement of labour and management in the economic and social decisions of the Community.

The change in direction can be attributed to several factors. The entry into government or coalition of Socialist parties in many countries brought about a new alignment of forces, in which the West Germans played a conspicuous part. The prospective enlargement of the Community with the entry of Britain, Ireland and Denmark was another factor in stressing social policies.

Many people within the EEC leadership were increasingly coming to realize the need to command wider support for the idea of European Community among the general population of the Nine, particularly after the result of the Norwegian referendum and the negative attitude adopted by the trade union and labour movement in Britain in 1972.

The trade union movements in the original six countries had long been pressing for the adoption of more dynamic and effective social policies and had been urging that trade unionists should have a bigger voice in Community affairs. As recently as May 1972, the assembly of the world Christian organization (World Confederation of Labour) passed a resolution calling for the 'democratization' of the Community, the strengthening of its Economic and Social Committee and the introduction of a direct system of consultation with European trade unions. Similar demands have been voiced by unions within the International Confederation of Free Trade Unions.

The Paris declaration was warmly welcomed in most trade union circles and, indeed, throughout the Community. One commentator described it as 'the Community's New Testament, with the original Rome Treaty as the Old.' It gave the green light to those concerned with social and regional planning to engage in a determined attempt to speed progress towards achieving the Community aims of improving living and working conditions.

Before describing these plans, contained in the Commission's 'social action programme', it is necessary to make a brief review of the principal institutions of the EEC, which have a bearing on economic and social policy.

Principal EEC Institutions

The supreme policy-making authority in the EEC is the Council of Ministers, attended by foreign ministers or ministers concerned with particular subjects under discussion, on the basis of one per member state. It usually meets in Brussels, and its sessions take up about 80 days a year. Voting is generally by a majority, but some decisions require a qualified majority with weighted voting and need at least 41 out of a total of 58 votes. This procedure is often avoided by means of a compromise or 'consensus' decision.

Decisions of the Council are carried out by the European Commission, which also has to initiate and prepare proposals for the Council's approval. Neither the Council nor the Commission has the power to enforce a decision — this is the responsibility of individual member states. Disputes over the application or interpretation of Community rules are referred to the European Court of Justice, which sits in Luxembourg.

According to the Treaty (articles 189-192) the Council and the Commission carry out their task by means of regulations, directives, decisions, recommendations or opinions. Regulations are binding in each member state. Directives are binding in content, but the method of application is left to individual member choice. Decisions are binding in entirety. Recommendations and opinions have no binding force.

The Commission, following the enlargement of the Community, is composed of 13 members. They are responsible to the EEC and not to any member state and each is assigned a special portfolio. During 1973 the Commission consisted of the following members:

President:
  François-Xavier Ortoli (French)
Vice-Presidents:
  Wilhelm Haferkamp (German) Finance and economic affairs
  Carlo Scarascia-Mugnozza (Italian) Parliamentary relations, transport, environment, consumer and information
  Sir Christopher Soames (British) External relations
  Dr Patrick Hillery (Irish) Social policy
  Henri Simonet (Belgian) Fiscal affairs and energy
Members:
  Jean-François Deniau (French) Development and budget and financial control
  Altiero Spinelli (Italian) Industry and technology
  Albert Borschette (Luxembourg) Competition, personnel
  Ralf Dahrendorf (German) Research, science and education
  George Thomson (British) Regional policy
  P. J. Lardinois (Dutch) Agriculture
  F. O. Gundelach (Danish) Internal market, customs union

The oldest European institution is the European Coal and Steel Community, set up in the early 1950s on the initiative of France's then foreign minister, Robert Schuman. The ECSC has its own institutions, based in Luxembourg, and provided the springboard for later and wider Common Market development.

The functioning of the European Parliament is outside the scope of this book but it is worth noting that there is strong pressure from EEC labour movements to strengthen its influence, and thereby inject more democracy into the proceedings of the Commission. In the past it has largely been a 'talking-shop', but particularly with the arrival of British MPs (though not Labour), it has taken on a more vigorous life. European trade unionists have established direct links with the parliamentary parties with which their movements are associated.

The most important EEC organization in the social field is its Economic and Social Committee, established under the Rome Treaty. It is an advisory body, but according to the Treaty, it must be consulted on major matters of economic and social policy which are specifically laid down in the Treaty (for example agriculture, free movement of labour, transport) and on other subjects as appropriate.

The Committee consists of 144 members — 24 each from Germany, France, Italy and the UK; 12 each from Belgium and the Netherlands; 9 each from Denmark and Ireland and 6 from Luxembourg. Members, who hold office for four years, are chosen by the Council of Ministers on an individual basis. They represent the interests of agriculture, industry, workpeople, the liberal professions and 'other' (mainly consumer) groups. The Committee holds a general assembly and is subdivided into 9 special committees:

1 Agriculture
2 Transport
3 Economic and finance
4 Social
5 Industrial and commercial
6 Foreign relations
7 Energy
8 Regional development and environment
9 Health

Other groups can be added as necessary. It is administered by an executive bureau, with a secretariat under a secretary-general.

The Economic and Social Committee is a somewhat unwieldy and slow-moving body and, largely because of this, its recommendations are not always acted upon by Ministers.

From time to time the Commission arranges special employment or industrial and social conferences. It recently set up a standing committee on employment, on which employers and unions are represented, with the object of coordinating labour policies throughout the Community. This committee is regularly consulted before proposals on employment policy are reached.

An important EEC instrument is its social fund. This was originally established in 1958 to help member countries by providing half the costs in retraining redundant workers. Between 1958 and 1971, nearly 1.5 million workers were helped through the fund, which received grants of £110 million in all. In the early 1970s, plans were approved after long discussion to increase the effectiveness of the fund. It was reformed in May 1972 to enable it to launch training and retraining schemes for workers before they lost their jobs, and to help with the restructuring of industry and the creation of new employment opportunities in areas vulnerable to unemployment. For 1973, the fund was allocated grants of about £150 million over a three-year period, of which nearly half was to be spent in the first year. There is a social fund committee, on which employers and workers are represented.

Another significant development was the decision to establish in 1973 a special regional fund (of about £200 million). Originally the development of regional policies and measures to counter unemployment in the poorer areas was left to individual member states but, in the early 1970s, increasing priority was given to direct action by the Commission with the object of taking work to the workers, rather than workers to the work and reducing the volume of mass emigration to richer areas as a result of economic pressure.

Imbalances are most marked in Britain, Italy and Ireland, all of which can expect eventually to benefit from the EEC policies, even though a period of intensive and tough bargaining about the allocation of resources seems inevitable. The European Investment Bank, set up under the Rome Treaty, provides another channel for regional aid, by investing in infrastructural development and new technological activities.

It is hardly surprising that with this cumbersome and complex machinery, and the paraphernalia of consultative committees and counter-balances, it takes time for policies which are hatched in the EEC offices at Brussels to reach fruition. Differences in language, traditions and customs make it difficult for the staffs and representatives of the new countries to adjust to patterns which were established 15 years ago and which are largely unchanged. But certainly the men and women who work in the divisions headed by Patrick Hillery and George Thomson (social affairs and regional development respectively) are concerned about the need for speed in implementing their ideas.

In the comparatively short time between the summit conference in October 1972 and April 1973, the Commission presented to the Council of Ministers an interim 'Social action' programme, designed to implement the

Paris declaration and to form the basis of a future 'social charter' for the Community.

The idea of centralized solutions is ruled out, as incompatible with national traditions and development, but the Commission suggests several fields where the EEC could take action to promote social progress. The three main priorities are:

1   Full and better employment.
2   Improved living and working conditions.
3   Worker participation in economic and social decision-making.

Proposals under these three headings include:

(a) Community contributions to employment premiums for the creation of new jobs in backward or declining areas.
(b) Help with retraining schemes, with guarantees against loss of income.
(c) Establishment of a European centre for vocational training.
(d) Better social benefits, education and housing for migrant workers.
(e) More job opportunities for women and school-leavers.
(f) Special aid for elderly and handicapped workers.
(g) Permanent links between the Commission and national employment services, with better coordination of statistics, and the standardization of information.

The Commission proposes to examine such questions as minimum wages, progress with equal pay, the workers' share in capital formation, and unemployment benefit schemes. It plans to launch pilot housing schemes and to carry out research into ways of overcoming the monotony of work on assembly lines.

As far as worker participation in decision-making is concerned, the Commission's proposals are discussed on pages 30-1. The Commission also aims to bring trade unions more closely into EEC affairs by strengthening the standing committee on employment, holding special labour conferences and providing regular information to European unions on EEC matters.

The Commission aimed to issue its final plan in the autumn of 1973 when it hoped to secure the approval of the Council of Ministers for a major campaign during 1974.

3

International Organizations

Trade Unions

There is a long and deep-rooted tradition of international solidarity in the trade unions, although it was slower to develop organizationally than in the political fields. The first international trade secretariats, linking unions in the same craft or industry, were set up towards the end of the nineteenth century, though some European craftsmen, for example, the glove-makers, established mutual links as early as 1860. An International Trade Union Secretariat was created in Copenhagen in 1903 with headquarters in Berlin and, on the eve of the First World War, it was transformed into the International Federation of Trade Unions (IFTU).

The IFTU was active in the immediate postwar period, particularly in connection with the foundation of the International Labour Organization. It was, from the outset, an essentially European body, representing the interests of workers in industrially developed countries. Between the wars, the IFTU experienced political and religious divisions.

In the early 1920s the Communists broke away to form their own Third International and the Christians also established an international organization. The IFTU was further weakened when the growth of Fascism led to the progressive loss of member organizations in Italy, Germany, Austria and Spain.

The outbreak of the Second World War put an end to formal international trade union activities (although a skeleton organization continued to operate). As soon as the war ended attempts were made to reconstruct the movement. In the euphoric atmosphere following victory in Europe and the foundation of the United Nations, the trade unions catering for both Communists and non-Communists joined together to establish the World Federation of Trade Unions. The unity, forged in London in 1945, was short-lived and could not survive the Cold War. The WFTU split in 1949 and the non-Communists formed their own body — the International Confederation of Free Trade Unions (ICFTU). In 1968, the Christians reorganized their international, under the title World Confederation of Labour (WCL).

The world labour scene is now dominated by three major organizations:

1   The International Confederation of Free Trade Unions (ICFTU).
2   The World Federation of Trade Unions (WFTU).
3   The World Confederation of Labour (WCL).

International Confederation of Free Trade Unions

The ICFTU initially claimed unions representing 48 million workers in 69 organizations in 53 countries. At the July 1972 congress, the ICFTU had a membership of 51.5 million workers in 113 organizations in 89 countries.

Its headquarters are in Brussels, with David MacDonald (Canada) as president and Otto Kersten (Germany) as general secretary. Many of its principal affiliates are socialist-orientated, but membership is open to any bona fide organization, so long as it is independent of outside domination and its leaders are democratically elected. The main slogan of the ICFTU is 'Bread, peace and freedom'.

The eight basic aims of the ICFTU are:

1   To promote the interests of working people everywhere.
2   To work for rising living standards and full employment.
3   To reduce the gap between rich and poor, within and between nations.
4   To work for international understanding, disarmament and the establishment of peace.
5   To help to organize the workers and secure union recognition as free bargaining agents.
6   To support the right to democratic elections.
7   To fight against oppression and discrimination.
8   To defend the fundamental human and trade union rights.

The ICFTU supreme authority is its congress, which meets every 3 years and elects an executive board, which meets at least twice a year and elects the president and vice-presidents. The ICFTU has regional organizations in Asia, Africa, and the Americas.

World Federation of Trade Unions

The WFTU is based in Prague, its European membership consists of trade unions in the USSR and East European Communist countries, together with the French CGT and the Italian CGIL. It claims 155 million members in 53 countries (10 in Africa, 12 in Latin America, 17 in Asia and 13 in Europe, 1 in Australasia). The WFTU aims are:

1   To consolidate and unite the unions of the world, irrespective of race, nationality, religion or politics.
2   To encourage the systematic exchange of information and experience.
3   To help the workers to organize unions.
4   To promote training.
5   To increase class-consciousness.
6   To represent workers interests in international organizations.

Its congress meets every 4 years and elects a general council, which meets every year. The executive bureau meets three times a year. The secretary-general is Pierre Gensous (France).

World Confederation of Labour

The WCL started as a European organization in 1920 and assumed its present title in 1968. The WCL too organizes workers in the developing countries. Its message is addressed to 'workers everywhere in the world who are willing to subscribe to its principles, whatever their creed, concept of life, race or sex'. The WCL congress meets every 4 years, the confederation board annually. It claims a membership of about 5 million.

Links between the Organizations

All three international bodies have consultative status *vis-à-vis* such international bodies as the ILO and the UN Economic and Social Council. The ICFTU has ruled out any organizational links with WFTU. As a statement issued after its executive meeting in July 1973 put it: 'The ICFTU's basic principles do not allow for any relationship with international or regional bodies whose policies are in diametrical conflict with free and democratic trade union objectives . . .' However, it did not rule out the establishment of bilateral contacts between individual organizations.

Both ICFTU and WCL have links with their respective international trade secretariats, or bodies based on specific industries. In the ICFTU these are autonomous bodies, but they accept the principles and policy of the ICFTU and are represented on its various committees. There are 16 international trade secretariats (building, clerical, chemical, diamond, entertainment, food, printing, metalworking, petroleum, agricultural, postal, public services, shoe and leather, teachers, textile and garment, transport). The most important are the International Metalworkers' Federation (IMF) with nearly 11 million members in 59 countries; the International Transport Workers' Federation (ITF) 6.5 million in 81 countries; Miners International Federation (MIF), 2 million members in 32 countries; International Federation of Chemical and General Workers' Unions (ICF) 3 million members in 60 countries; The Public Services International (PSI), 3.7 million members in 64 countries; International Federation of Commercial, Clerical and Technical Employees (FIET), 5.5 million members in 70 countries.

All the international trade secretariats hold congresses, usually every 3-4 years, and include among their objectives, exchanging information, representing their industrial members' interests in various international bodies, encouraging union membership, helping organizations, coordinating activities and supporting individual unions in the event of disputes — this has been particularly effective in the case of the IMF and the ITF.

European Organizations

European Confederation of Free Trade Unions

ICFTU unions in the original six EEC countries established an organization which started as an informal secretariat and later became known as the European Confederation of Free Trade Unions (ECFTU). The initiative for its formation came from miners and steelworkers in 1949, at the time of the establishment of the European Coal and Steel Community, in which unions had very early on established their right to representation. After the signature of the Treaty of Rome, the organization extended its scope to present a counterweight to the business and industrial forces which dominated the EEC. ECFTU played a major part in pressing for union representation on the various committees of the Commission and in demanding more democratic and dynamic social policies. In an action programme, adopted in May 1965, it called for the introduction throughout the Six of a 40-hour week, 4 weeks paid holiday, improved holiday pay and security of income for disabled workers.

ICFTU unions also participated in a committee for the European Free Trade Association (EFTA) set up in the 1960s. The British and Scandinavian unions were the dominant members of this group.

European Trade Union Confederation

With the prospect of the enlargement of the EEC and the growing size of industrial units, the ECFTU and the committee for EFTA felt that the time was ripe to increase their impact by joining forces. After complex and delicate negotiations which began in the early 1970s, the European Trade Union Confederation (ETUC) was formed. The formal foundation ceremony took place in Brussels in February 1973. It was attended by representatives of ECFTU unions and of unions in EFTA countries (including the UK and Denmark, which joined the EEC in January 1973, but excluding Ireland, which is not affiliated to ICFTU, and Portugal) plus the clandestine Spanish Unión General de Trabajadores. Vic Feather, general secretary of the British TUC until September 1973, was elected president and Theo Rasschaert of Belgium its general secretary.

The ETUC comprises 17 national federations with a total of 29 million workers, and representing about one in three of all the workers in the member countries. The founding members are affiliated to the ICFTU and support its objectives but the ETUC is a separate organizational entity.

Its congress, scheduled to meet every 3 years, elects an executive, in which each organization has one member, apart from Britain and Germany which have two. Industrial trade groups are represented but do not have voting rights.

The purpose of the Confederation, set out in its constitution is to 'represent and promote the social, economic and cultural intersts of workers at the European level in general, and in particular in respect of all European institutions, including the European Communities and the EFTA'.

The Confederation's leaders are determined that the new body should not be just a talking-shop, expressing pious hopes of European solidarity. They believe that it should take the lead in and coordinate activities designed to give European workers a bigger voice in European institutions and further social and regional development. They are anxious to dispel fears that the ETUC might develop into a European club for the more wealthy unions and have stressed from the outset that aid to developing nations remains a paramount objective.

The Christians' European Organization

The Christian Confederation decided in 1958 to establish its own European organization (now EO–WCL). This consists of national confederations mainly from Belgium, France, the Netherlands and Switzerland. It is associated with international trade or professional bureaux which include the following: general, metal, public service, transport, textile and garment, food, hotel, agriculture, white-collar and administrative, print and paper, teaching, wood and building. EO–WCL'S congress meets every 3 years and it has a directing committee, an executive bureau and a permanent secretariat. EO–WCL's constitution describes it as an organization of national confederations specifically based on 'Christian social principles' and other organizations which accept these principles. Its president is J. Hout Huis (Belgium). The organization in 1966 set out the guiding lines for the organization – European unification, unity of action while retaining separate identities and maximum pressure to secure representation for the workers in Europe.

At its congress in May 1972, the organization set out new objectives, in which unity of trade union action in Europe was given pride of place. It emphasized the need for economic and social integration within the EEC and developing its social programme, with a view to the eventual drawing up of collective European agreements.

Individual Unions' Attitudes towards EEC

The unions in the original six EEC countries which are affiliated to the ICFTU have always supported the Common Market and are agreed in demanding that the Community should give higher priority to social reform and that unions should have a stronger say in EEC institutions. The Germans constituted the biggest single union block within the original EEC and succeeded in enlisting the backing of the Commission for worker participation plans on their own 'Mitbestimmung' lines. In France, the various union centres were divided at the outset. The CGT initially declared its open hostility to the Common Market, but later accepted the reality of its existence; the Socialist and former Christian groups have all along backed the concept. In Italy, likewise, the Christian and social-democratic centres have always given full support to European institutions. The Communist-led CGIL, though it originally condemned the Community as a reactionary 'monopolists' set-up, toned down its opposition. The Italian and French Communist-led centres have established a permanent committee to represent their interests *vis-à-vis* the Community; their representatives sit on the Economic and Social Committee and are demanding full participation.

The Irish TUC was originally against the EEC, but since a national referendum produced a majority in favour, Irish trade unionists have been participating fully in EEC committee work.

In Britain, the TUC was originally, on balance, pro-European and supported the Wilson government's move to reopen negotiations on British entry in 1967. But its attitude changed and, in 1972, the Congress carried two resolutions, one opposing membership and the other calling for the renegotiation of entry terms. The TUC General Council decided therefore not to send representatives to the EEC committees, such as the Economic and Social Committee. At the same time, many individual British unions, including miners, steelworkers and workers in shipping and aviation, made their independent links with their opposite numbers in the EEC countries. The TUC boycott caused deep disappointment among European unions and in April 1973 the European Trade Union Confederation, of which Vic Feather is president, wrote to him as TUC general secretary deploring the nonrepresentation of British trade unionists on the Economic and Social Committee, while British employers were represented. The General Council took the line that it was up to individual unions to make their own decision in their specialist fields, but that the TUC itself was bound by the 1972 decision. This was reaffirmed at the 1973 Congress.

Employers' Organizations

The main international employers' organization is the International Organization of Employers (IOE). It was founded in Washington in 1919, during the first International Labour Conference and has remained the spokesman for employers at the ILO and other United Nations bodies. Originally it was concerned only with industrial employers but in 1948 it enlarged its scope to include all employers. Its main objects are to act as a clearing house for information for its members and to assist them to resolve social and labour problems. IOE has a general council which elects an executive committee and has a staff of 11. Its headquarters are in Geneva. Its secretary-general is Monsieur R. Lagasse. The organization comprises 87 employers' federations in 77 countries.

In Europe, employers are organized in the Union des Industries de la Communauté Européenne (UNICE). This was set up in 1958 and consisted of the main employers' organizations of the six, which were joined in 1973 by those of the three new entrants to the EEC. Its main object is to speak for industry *vis-à-vis* Common Market institutions and to 'encourage the elaboration of an industrial policy in a European spirit'.

The decision-making body of UNICE is its council of presidents and its day-to-day affairs are run by the general secretary with a staff.

There is a committee of permanent delegates which meets two or three times a month and there are about 30 different committees and working parties dealing with particular aspects of the EEC. Its general secretary is Miss H. M. Claessens.

UNICE is not a negotiating body; it is essentially a pressure group for industry within the EEC, as well as providing its constituent members with factual information about Common Market policies and plans. UNICE is non-political and, in general, supports the system of free enterprise, with the minimum of government interference in industry. In May 1973 it issued a memorandum on 'social policy in Europe'.

In this memorandum, UNICE accepted that both sides of industry should have an increasing share in EEC social decisions and that social aspects of European integration should receive greater consideration. It urged the need for national governments to coordinate their social policies in the interests of harmonization. It accepted the idea of European-level industrial relations, but rejected the view that employers should bear an increasing burden of the costs of social security by means of indirect wages.

4

Some Major Issues for European Unions

Whatever the differences in their organization and in the methods they adopt to realize their objectives, there are many common problems facing the European trade union movements. It is indeed largely to resolve these problems that the unions have created a European organization, on the basis that through their combined weight they can exert a stronger influence on employers and on the various European institutions.

Two major and controversial issues dominated the scene in the early 1970s; the subjects were workers' participation and the growth of multinational companies. Among many other common issues were the position of migrant labour, equal pay for men and women and the 'quality' of working life. The above five issues are dealt with in this chapter. The overriding economic problems of inflation, expansion and fiscal controls, though of paramount concern to workers, have been omitted as being altogether too complex a subject for summarizing and being the responsibility of governments rather than trade unions.

Workers' Participation

Industrial democracy, in the sense of giving workers a bigger say in and control over the management of their industrial and working lives, has long been an objective of trade unions. In the EEC countries, unions have succeeded, to a greater or lesser degree, in making progress towards their goal; the position in individual countries is described later in this book. Here the situation is considered in its European context.

The European Commission brought the issue to the forefront with two distinct, but related, proposals. First, the draft statute for a European company was produced in 1970, as a possible blueprint for companies operating as European organizations within the Community. The proposed statute is not mandatory. It suggests that a European company should have three governing bodies: a general meeting (equivalent to a shareholders' meeting) a supervisory board and a board of management. The supervisory board would exercise overall control over policy and supervise the management board, which would remain responsible for day-to-day administration. It is proposed that two-thirds of the members of the supervisory board would be appointed by the general meeting and that the remaining third would consist of workers' representatives, appointed by the company's employees — normally nominated by the works council.

This system is akin to the German practice in private industry, but in Britain there is no equivalent two-tier division in companies of supervisory and managerial functions. In Britain works councils operate on a voluntary, not statutory basis as they do in Germany.

The statute also proposes that a European company should have a European works council representing the workers in each of the company's plants. A European works council would be set up in every European company with establishments in more than one European state. It would not be a negotiating body, but it would have general responsibility for looking after the workers' interests, enable them to receive information about the current situation and future plans of the company and give workers the right to be consulted on decisions affecting to their employment and working conditions. Seven subjects are listed as questions on which the board of management could only make decisions with the agreement of the works council — recruitment, promotion and dismissals, vocational training, terms of remuneration, safety and health, social facilities, hours and holidays.

Second, and more important, is the Commission's draft fifth directive on company law, circulated at the end of September 1972. This would be mandatory and would cover all sociétés anonymes — or equivalent business organizations, such as public limited companies in the UK — with more than 500 employees.

The draft directive repeats the plan for company structure outlined in the draft company statute — general meeting, supervisory board and management board — with workers on the supervisory board, representing at least one-third of the membership. The directive suggests two alternative means by which the principle could be achieved — the appointment by the workers of at least one-third (the German system) or by cooption for the whole supervisory board, including workers' representatives (the Dutch system).

The attitudes of various trade union bodies to the fifth directive varies widely. In Germany, as might be expected, the DGB is strongly in favour of the plan, which is largely based on the German model of 'Mitbestimmung'. The unions would however like to see parity of representation for workers and shareholders on the supervisory board, as in the European Coal and Steel Community. Dutch trade unions broadly support the plan and so does the Danish LO, though it proposes that workers should elect two members of the supervisory board in companies with more than 50 workers.

In France and Italy, where Communist influence is strong, opinions are divided. The CGT, committed to the overthrow of capitalism, is against both worker participation on company boards and works councils. The other two main union centres, Force ouvrière and the CFDT broadly favour the European scheme for works councils but are suspicious of board representation. Considerable interest has been expressed in Italy, where the main union centres are engaged in discussions on unification.

Opinion is divided in Belgium. The Christians accept the idea of the increased involvement of workers in management but the Socialist FGTB, which believes that 'the aims of the capitalistic system are incompatible with those of the trade unions' advocate workers' control as the real solution.

British trade union thinking has undergone a radical change in recent years. In an interim report in January 1973 and a discussion paper on industrial democracy in August 1973, the TUC accepted the idea of two-tier boards as 'probably a desirable development', and agreed with the principle of worker representation on the supervisory board. It insisted, however, that workers representatives should be trade union members, elected through trade union machinery and responsible to trade unionists in the firm rather than to the general meeting. It considered that workers should occupy half the seats on these boards, and not the one-third suggested by the EEC, and that the EEC directive should apply to firms with 200 and not 500 employees. Worker representatives should have the right of appointment or veto of certain members of the managerial board.

The TUC is more dubious about the proposal for a European works council, which 'has to be looked at very carefully'. Since there is no statutory machinery for works councils in Britain, appointments would need to be made through the appropriate trade union machinery in British subsidiaries. However, it agrees that such a council might perform a useful function in providing for some multinational union control over certain decisions of multinational companies.

Generally speaking, European employers' organizations accept the idea of increased worker participation in industry, but they would prefer to see this exercised through works councils rather than by direct worker representation on supervisory boards. Thus the UNICE (European employers' organization) in a statement in May 1973 pronounced itself in favour of the maximum 'dialogue' between employers and workers and the interchange of information, but considered this was best left on a flexible basis, without formal regulation.

In Britain, the Engineering Employers Federation came out (May 1973) with bitter opposition to the introduction of the German-type scheme in England.

> It leans heavily on a range of assumptions that simply do not hold water in the British industrial relations and financial environment. Its major proposals are altogether unsuitable for grafting on to United Kingdom practice . . . The best prospect for securing meaningful participation lies in the encouragement of consultation and two-way communication.

The draft fifth directive has been debated in the European Parliament and the governments of EEC countries were collecting and collating the views of the interested parties. It will inevitably take a long time and a great deal of debate before the Commission's proposals leave the drawing-board stage.

Multinational Companies

The development of cross-frontier trade union cooperation to counter the growth of multinational companies started in the late 1960s and gathered momentum during the early 1970s. Multinationals became one of the most important issues on the international labour scene.

There is no precise definition of the term 'multinational'. Broadly, it is taken to include any company which has headquarters in one country and carries out operational activities in another. Multinational companies, or corporations, are usually very large and are found in capital-intensive industries. The most powerful groups are American-owned — General Motors, Ford, Esso, Chrysler, ITT, Du Pont, Kodak, Standard Oil and Westinghouse are among the best-known. European-owned multinationals include Royal Dutch/Shell, Unilever, ICI, Volkswagen, Philips, British Leyland, Fiat, Nestlé, Siemens, Hoechst and Thyssen.

The majority of multinational companies operate in engineering, automobiles, electronics, petroleum, chemicals and food production.

Trade unions recognize the economic reasons for the development of worldwide industrial enterprise. A resolution adopted at an ICFTU congress in Brussels in 1969 stated that 'the international organization of production can play an important role in spreading new technical know-how and in giving an impetus to economic growth and social progress'.

Mr Vic Feather, TUC general secretary, at a special conference on international companies in October 1970, said that the TUC was not opposed to foreign takeovers as such.

> We are neither against nor for it [the international company] as such. We recognize that the mushrooming of the multinational corporation is a fact of life in the international economic reality of the second half of this century.

Trade unions, however, insist that they should have the opportunity to safeguard the interests of both the workers within the company and the general public and call on governments to scrutinize carefully all proposals for takeovers.

The ICFTU has identified several grounds for union fears. Multinational corporations, said the Brussels 1969 resolution, could pose a new challenge by:

1 Jeopardizing democratic national planning in individual countries.
2 Undermining local systems of industrial relations — since decision-making is centralized in one place.
3 Arbitrarily transferring resources from one country to another.
4 Adopting anti-union policies and limiting the right of collective bargaining.
5 Exploiting international labour cost differentials in order to increase their profits.

The ICFTU therefore called on workers to unite to meet the challenge and to demand the right of union recognition and collective bargaining, in line with ILO conventions. It urged public authorities to ensure that national economic and social needs were safeguarded and emphasized the need for democratic control and accountability at each level of decision-making.

The 1969 policy was reaffirmed and strengthened at subsequent ICFTU conferences. The Christian International (WCL) and the World Federation of Trade Unions (WFTU) have likewise expressed concern at the possible dangers presented by the multinationals. In the autumn of 1972 the ILO held a conference representing governments, employers and workers to discuss the relationship between multinationals and social policy and embarked on a study in depth of this problem.

At a meeting in Brussels in 1973, an ICFTU working party on multi-national companies agreed to seek a common international strategy and stressed that the main priority must be research. This would cover such questions as:

1   The effect of multinational companies on the economy of developing countries and on the employment situation.
2   The problem of securing a greater measure of industrial democracy.
3   The legal aspects of trade union action across frontiers.
4   The possibility of drawing up an international code of conduct.
5   A blacklist of persistent anti-union companies.

The practical problem facing trade union negotiators is a very real one. When they deal with the top management of a national company (that is, a company that only operates in one country), they meet face-to-face round the negotiating table, thrash out their problems and probably arrive at an immediate decision. When they deal with the subsidiary of a multinational company, they are not talking to the fountainhead of authority – decisions are taken elsewhere and the local manager may be as ignorant of the company's long-term strategy as the trade unionist. If a union threatens industrial action, the company can switch production to another plant, build up stockpiles or even threaten to close down and move to an area where the labour force is more amenable. This may not always be feasible, but the threat is a real one. A multinational management is in a position to select its most advantageous industrial location and to build up investment in the areas which it regards as most favourable. Unions can usually find out a certain amount about the plans of a national company, but in the case of multinationals, knowledge resides with the central management and the unions are kept in the dark about future plans. This is particularly the case with the large motor corporations like Ford and General Motors, where major investment decisions are taken on the other side of the Atlantic.

There is scope for bilateral action between unions representing workers in the same company. Thus, in 1967, the American United Automobile Workers were able to secure wage parity for the Canadian and American employees of Chrysler and in 1969, during a strike at Ford's Belgian plant at Genk, near the German border, German workers refused to be used as substitute labour or to allow work from Belgium to be switched to Germany. More recently, shop stewards of Dunlop-Pirelli in Italy and Britain took joint action over threatened redundancies.

The main vehicles for international union cooperation are the international trade secretariats (see pages 23-4). Their activities in relation to multinational companies were summarized in a TUC report of 1970 as being:

1 Research and the collection of information.
2 International organization of unions in standing bodies representing employees working for the same company.
3 International solidarity and aid, for example, financial support for unions in dispute.
4 Multinational consultation with managements over a wide range of issues other than collective bargaining, including advance warning of plans to transfer production.
5 Synchronization of the timing of claims and common termination dates of existing and future collective agreements in the subsidiaries concerned.
6 Coordination of industrial action.
7 Harmonization of collective bargaining objectives, other than wages.
8 Harmonization of collective bargaining on wages.
9 Presentation of internationally agreed demands to multinational companies as a whole and coordination of tactics to realize these.

The largest and most powerful ITS, the International Metalworkers, has been the pacemaker. As long ago as 1964 it organized special conferences, largely on the initiative of the late Walter Reuther, President of the UAW (United Auto, Aircraft and Agricultural Implements Workers of America), which led to the establishment of world autoworkers councils. These were set up for Ford, General Motors, Chrysler, Volkswagen, Fiat-Citroën in 1966 and for Nissan-Toyota, BLMS-Renault-Volvo in 1968. The councils act as a clearinghouse for factual information and cooperate to bring pressure on the companies concerned. The IMF, based in Geneva, has built up an impressive dossier of research into wages and working conditions in car plants all over the world. It is particularly concerned about operations in the developing countries of Latin America and Asia, and in low-wage areas and countries such as Spain where there is no democratic trade union movement.

Union pressure has, on many occasions, been successfully brought to bear on subsidiaries in developing countries, for example, Argentina and Chile, to win union recognition and the right of collective bargaining.

Mr Daniel Benedict, assistant general secretary of the IMF, stated

> The challenge of multinational companies has led to the first new
> structural adaptation of international trade unionism in decades; the
> formation of world councils or working parties of workers in specific
> companies around the globe.

For Europe, there is a separate body — the European Metalworkers
Federation (EMF). It is not a regional organization of the IMF, though the
two organizations work in close association. The EMF operates exclusively
within the EEC countries. The EMF has defined its three main tasks as
being:

1   To achieve common action of all metalworkers in the Community.
2   To represent their interests within the EEC.
3   To negotiate with European employers and with the head offices of
    multinational companies operating in the EEC.

The EMF has made most progress in its discussions with the Philips
electrical concern at Eindhoven, Holland. Regular meetings have been held
since 1967 and a council has been formed which meets once a year. The
Philips management has accepted the unions right to discuss matters of
common interest affecting its European operations such as company policy
on personnel, profits, etc; to provide the unions with information and give
advance warning about plans affecting future employment prospects.

Talks have covered such subjects as shift working and job security,
training and retraining, policies on wages and working conditions, harmonization of fringe benefits, coordination of social welfare plans as well as
the general economic and financial situation.

As yet, the stage of international collective bargaining has not been
reached, but the Philips example of consultation and information-giving is
one that provides an excellent pattern for future relations between a
multinational company and trade unions.

The EMF has also had discussions with Metal Packaging, Fokker/VFW,
(the German-Dutch aircraft company,) Fiat, Citroën-Berliet and Airbus-
Concorde groups.

The essence of its operations is speed in identifying disputed points and
arranging for information to be disseminated to shop stewards and other
workers' representatives who are affected by the outcome of the talks.

Apart from the activities of the International Federation of Chemical and

General Workers' Unions, other international trade secretariats have also been concerned with multinational problems. The International Federation of Commercial, Clerical and Technical Employees (FIET) has had talks with IBM and has collected information on a global scale about comparative conditions, salaries, and profits in different international companies, which has been circulated to affiliates as an aid to negotiation.

The International Union of Food and Allied Workers' Associations (IUF) has organized conferences for workers employed by multinational concerns. For example, a conference of Nestlé employees held in May 1972 resulted in the setting up of a permanent council of Nestlé workers. According to the IUF, the company agreed to consider the IUF as a bona fide representative of its employees at the international level and gave 'certain assurances concerning its general labour policies and agreed in principle to see that its subsidiaries would follow general guidelines'. The IUF intervened in a dispute over union recognition involving Nestlé's subsidiary in Peru which occurred in the spring of 1973. Many unions sent financial aid and the strike was settled when the management agreed to recognize the unions.

The IUF has set up a permanent world council for the W.R. Grace and Company food and chemical concern but the company has declined to divulge information about its future plans for plant closures. The IUF has also had dealings with the International Sleeping-Car and Tourist Company, British American Tobacco and Coca-Cola. In June 1973 it established an international council representing Unilever workers.

Collective international action *vis-à-vis* multinational companies is still in an embryonic stage and there is, as yet, no sign of firm progress towards collective bargaining on a multinational basis. This, however, is the long-term objective of the unions. As Mr Otto Kersten, general secretary of the ICFTU, said in June 1973

> We must build up a trade union counterweight internationally to the multinational corporations, so that bargaining can be done in a coordinated fashion for all the workers of a multinational corporation.

Dr Patrick Hillery, a vice-president of the European Commission, has indicated that there is scope for Community action in the field of collective bargaining. He told the European parliament in January that the Commission could act as 'a clearinghouse for collective agreements on a European basis and the conclusion of European collective agreements could be considered'.

The employers' view, broadly, is that the idea of international collective bargaining is not realistic, owing to the wide differences in conditions and practices and the absence of any legalistic framework.

A fundamental difficulty lies in the difference in trade union structures and attitudes. People tend to think nationally rather than internationally and national unions are jealous of their independence. Workers are reluctant to become involved in disputes in other countries and there are real fears about job security. For example, leaders of British shipyard workers have expressed alarm about Fiat's reported plans to build a big marine engine plant at Trieste, which might endanger jobs in UK yards. In view of these attitudes, it is all the more remarkable that so much progress towards genuine international union cooperation has in fact been achieved.

Migrant Workers

Unemployment remained at a low level throughout the 1960s in the original six EEC countries, with the exception of Italy. There was a slight increase in Germany and France during 1970-71 but according to EEC sources the level dropped in most countries except France during 1972. In the three new entrants the highest unemployment level obtained in Ireland and the United Kingdom where it was exceeded only by Italy among the Six. Britain experienced a rapid fall in its level of unemployment during the second half of 1972 and the first half of 1973.

Most EEC countries suffered from a serious shortage of labour and filled the gap by importing foreign workers mainly from southern Mediterranean countries. About three million workers plus their families moved into EEC countries to find jobs. Although under the Treaty of Rome, EEC nationals are entitled to move about freely within the Community, in fact the intra-Community movement has been on a limited scale, apart from Italy, from which about one million workers emigrated.

The unemployment situation is shown in Figure 4:1 and the number of foreign workers in the EEC is shown in Figure 4:2.

The situation of the migrants, usually relegated to the more menial and uncongenial jobs which indigenous workers decline to accept in times of full employment and scarcity of skilled workers, has been causing concern to the Commission. Most migrants work in public service industries, domestic service, building, engineering and in the declining textile and mining industries. For the most part they live in overcrowded and unsatisfactory houses and are creating slum areas in and around the industrial centres. Few speak the language of their host country and education presents a serious problem. Mr Michael Shanks, chief of the social affairs division has written:-

From a social and a humanitarian point of view there is need for an urgent programme to improve conditions for Europe's six million or so migrant workers and their dependants. Otherwise there is a danger that migrant communities will come to form in Europe as in the US, cankers of poverty, misery and ignorance which will take generations to alleviate or eradicate.

Action to improve the position of migrant workers has therefore been given priority in the EEC social plan. It calls for the adoption by the end of 1974 of measures to extend full social protection to migrants, improved training, education, induction programmes and housing, as well as the opportunity for increasing participation in the economic, social and political life of the host country. The Commission has set up a tripartite committee on migrant workers.

Immigration is a problem for governments and public authorities rather than for trade unions. But unions clearly have an interest in ensuring that migrants do not become a threat to established wages and conditions and undermine social development. Union leaders from both emigrant and immigrant countries held a special conference on the subject in May 1973 and the ICFTU is planning a world conference in 1974. The general view is that more employment should be created in areas where unemployment is high in order to stem the tide of migration. A trade union charter is planned which will set out criteria for immigrants' conditions of work and life. The fact that many migrants have moved from their home countries on a

Figure 4:1 Unemployment

	Year	Belgium	Germany	France	Italy	Luxembourg
Unemployed	1958	3.4	2.9	1.0	(6.2)	0.0
as percentage of	1969	2.3	0.7	1.7	3.4	0.0
civilian labour	1970	2.0	0.6	1.7	3.2	0.0
force (unemployment rate)	1971	2.0	0.7	2.2	3.2	0.0

	Year	Netherlands	UK	Ireland	Denmark	TOTAL
Unemployed	1958	2.5	1.7	6.4	—	(3.0)
as percentage of	1969	1.5	2.0	5.2	1.1	1.9
civilian labour	1970	1.2	2.2	6.0	0.7	1.8
force (unemployment rate)	1971	1.5	2.9	6.0	1.2	2.1

Source: *Report on Social Situation in the Community 1972*, EEC, February 1973

Figure 4:2   Foreign workers in the EEC in April 1973

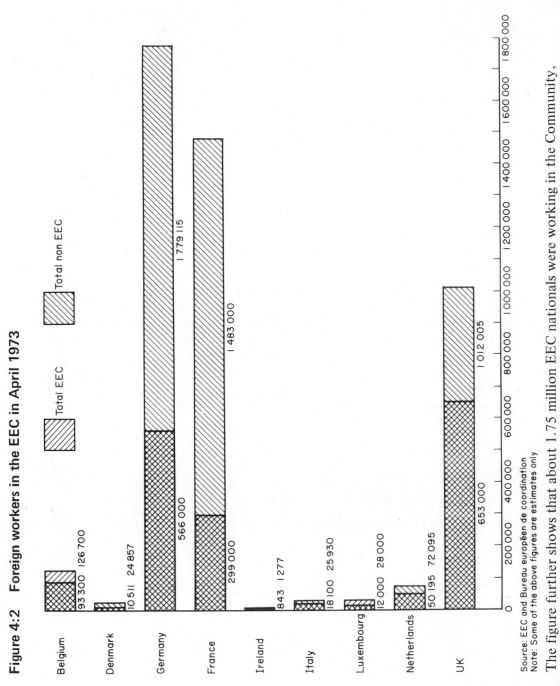

Total EEC

Total non EEC

	EEC	non EEC
Belgium	93 300	126 700
Denmark	10 511	24 857
Germany	566 000	1 779 115
France	299 000	1 483 000
Ireland	843	1 277
Italy	18 100	25 930
Luxembourg	12 000	28 000
Netherlands	50 195	72 095
UK	653 000	1 012 005

Source: EEC and Bureau européen de coordination
Note: Some of the above figures are estimates only

The figure further shows that about 1.75 million EEC nationals were working in the Community, compared with 4.5 million non EEC nationals, bringing the general total to 6.25 million.

short-term basis, rather than for permanent settlement, as well as differences in language, temperament and customs makes them difficult to organize. In some countries unions have tried to help the integration of foreign workers. For example, in Germany, they have issued newspapers and set up information bureaux. In Belgium, immigrant workers are effectively integrated into the trade union movement. On the whole, the reaction of the host country workers is passive rather than active. However, in Holland, trouble flared up in 1972 over the employment of Turkish workers, and in France, in March 1973, migrant workers at the Renault plant went on strike in protest against their conditions and lack of status.

Equal Pay

Women represent over half the total population of the EEC countries. The proportion who are in active employment varies considerably between the countries. The position in 1971 is shown in Figure 4:3.

Figure 4:3   Percentage of women in civilian employment in the EEC in 1971

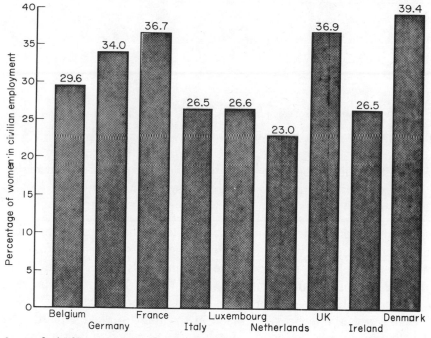

Source: *Social Situation in the Community*, 1972, EEC

In all the original six countries, the majority of working women are engaged in the tertiary sector, for example, services and clerical work and they account for a larger proportion of the workforce in this sector than men. (France 48.1 per cent, Germany 41.8 per cent, Belgium 38.7 per cent, Netherlands 32.8 per cent, Italy 30.9 per cent.) In industry, they are mainly engaged in textiles, clothing, food, electrical engineering etc. More than half the women at work are married, except in the Netherlands, where the proportion of married women working is just over 25 per cent.

The Treaty of Rome (article 119) lays down the principle 'that men and women should receive equal pay for equal work'. This principle is binding on member states, as is the ILO convention on equal pay but there is still a gap between men's and women's earnings although this has been progressively narrowed through collective bargaining.

Figure 4:4 shows the situation in various countries given in a report on equal pay by the Office of Manpower Economics (August 1972).

Figure 4:4   Average hourly earnings of women as a percentage of male average hourly earnings

	1964	1971
France	76	77
West Germany	69	70
Italy	70	76
Belgium	65	68
Luxembourg	45	56
Netherlands	56	61
UK*	57	59

*The Department of Employment points out that 'differences in overtime premia and shift premia, together with differences of definition, probably make it necessary to raise the UK percentage by several points in order to provide a reasonable basis for comparison with the other countries'.

A report sponsored by the Commission concluded that the application of the Rome Treaty remained 'a dead letter' in many countries and that the provision about equal pay tended to be 'meaningless'. The situation has improved since the publication of the report (1968) though full statistics have not become available. A report of the Commission in December 1972 referred to 'the irrefutable progress made in the field of wage equality'. It also drew attention to gaps and inadequacies and its main conclusion was:

Although undeniable progress has been made the situation is nevertheless still far from satisfactory. It therefore becomes absolutely essential that . . . a decisive impetus should be given in the search for a complete solution to this problem.

In most European countries, though not in Britain, there is a minimum legal wage which is the same for men and women. It is in *opportunity* for earnings that the inequalities arise and it is primarily through collective bargaining that progress will be made. In Belgium, the majority of women are protected by collective agreements, but in the Netherlands the proportion is as low as 20-25 per cent, and the basic wage is still lower for women than for men.

Direct discrimination has been diminishing, but indirect discrimination persists as a result of the reservation of special job categories for women and the underrating of women in general.

As the Commission has observed (June 1970) practices militating against equal pay include:

The systematic downgrading of women workers, the adoption of different qualification rules and the use of job evaluation not related to the real conditions in which the work is done.

Women tend to be concentrated in lower paid industries and jobs where they lack the opportunity to improve their skills. The disparity in skill is shown by the proportion of men and women classified as skilled in manufacturing industry in the original six EEC countries. (See Figure 4:5.)

It will be seen from Figure 4:5 that the gap is widest in Germany and Luxembourg (where few women are employed anyhow) and narrowest in Belgium and Italy.

Most EEC countries have some form of equal pay legislation or have built into their constitutions guarantees against discrimination on the grounds of sex. Only the Netherlands does not provide specific guarantees through legislation or its constitution, but there is no discrimination in its minimum wage legislation and in an increasing number of collective agreements. But, as the EEC has pointed out, there is considerable evasion of the law in many member states. The Commission decided in 1973 to take action against the Netherlands and Luxembourg for their failure to observe EEC regulations.

Most progress towards single classification schemes, irrespective of sex, has been made in Belgium, Italy and France. German unions maintain that the lowest categories are still reserved for women, though this is disputed by the

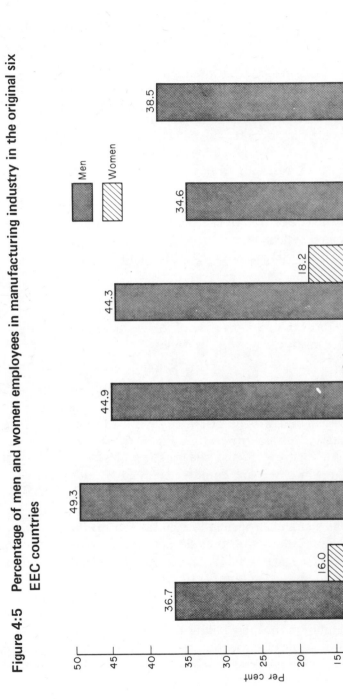

Figure 4:5   Percentage of men and women employees in manufacturing industry in the original six EEC countries

Men
Women

Source: Report of the Commission, June 1970

employers. In some companies, for example Philips, equality has been encouraged by the reduction in the number of categories.

In France, the CFDT consider that too much importance is attached in job classification to male qualities, for example strength, and not enough to female qualities, for example dexterity. The CGT has issued figures, showing a total number of women workers of just under six million in 1972. There was a gap of 23.3 per cent between the salaries of men and women white-collar workers and 30.3 per cent between the wages of men and women manual workers.

In Britain the Equal Pay Act was placed on the statute book in May 1970 and its full implementation is required before the end of December 1975. The terminology of the Act is slightly different from that in the Rome Treaty. The Act defines equality as applicable to 'work of the same or broadly similar nature to that of men, or work which has been given equal value under a job-evaluation scheme'. The Act (section 9) provided that if the Secretary of State for Employment was dissatisfied with progress at the half-way stage, he could make an order requiring women's rates to be raised to 90 per cent of men's. Because of its counter-inflation programme, the government did not make such an order, but suggested that the differential should be narrowed within the scope of the pay limits set under Stage Two of the programme. This was not satisfactory to the TUC which urged unions to continue to seek agreements which would give women at least 90 per cent of the men's rates.

In June 1973 the Department of Employment launched a special campaign to remind employers of their obligations under the Act. This included a personal letter from the Secretary of State for Employment to chairmen or managing directors of 400 000 firms.

The TUC, which has been pressing for equal pay since 1888, is also urging the need for special measures to help working mothers, such as more day nurseries and nursery schools and a greater flexibility in their working hours to fit their family commitments.

In Britain, as in all EEC countries, continuing pressure has been brought to bear by trade unions not only to close the pay gap, but to provide greater equality of opportunity for women, in whatever field they work. Here the Commission report concluded:

> Women continue to occupy the lowest posts in the hierarchy and the great majority of the female workforce is still concentrated in low-wage branches, in spite of the technological changes which have increased the interchangeability of men and women.

In its social plan, the Commission proposes to set up a permanent coordinating committee, pledged to report by the end of June 1974 on such questions as access to employment, promotion, training and retraining, maternity leave, child care facilities, working hours and social security provisions. This would form the basis for Commission proposals to the Council of Ministers.

The fact that in all EEC countries the proportion of women who belong to trade unions is low increases the difficulty of making progress towards equality and ensuring that they are not exploited.

Job Enrichment

Governments, managements, trade unionists, social scientists and workers themselves are becoming increasingly concerned about what might be called the 'quality' of working life, and about ways in which the monotony and boredom of repetitive and production-line jobs can be eliminated. The term 'job enrichment' has been used to describe this process. The term originated through the work of Frederick Herzberg, professor at Utah University, Salt Lake City and means 'motivating' workers to fulfil their potential. It is the direct antithesis of the Taylor principles of scientific management, first introduced in 1911. These meant that the worker had to work at a pace and for periods worked out by scientific methods, with the minimum training, though with opportunities for substantial bonuses. 'Taylorism' came to be associated primarily with assembly-line production in the car industry.

According to the Herzberg theory, it is essential to devise ways in which the worker's potential can be used and in which he can derive job satisfaction, becoming personally involved in production rather than an impersonal cog in the machine.

A number of significant experiments have already been conducted in America and in Europe. Some of these are described in a Department of Employment report *On the Quality of Working Life* by Dr N. A. B. Wilson, an industrial psychologist (June 1973). In Norway, for example, the manufacturing concern Norsk Hydro launched a project to increase productivity at its Eidanger fertilizer plant by a better use of human resources, cutting out rigid and de-skilled job assignments and detailed checking and regulation, and giving responsibility to a joint action group, including shop stewards and experienced operators, for planning the scheme. Rotation of jobs was arranged and the function of foremen and supervisors became advisory and consultative. After two years the experiment in one section proved so successful that it was extended to a further five sections.

The Philips group at Eindhoven, in the Netherlands, has conducted several experiments with turning the assembly line into team operations. At one factory, making electric heaters, there was a change from a conveyor-belt system to unit production by groups of workers. Output increased by 10 per cent and there was a 50 per cent reduction in faults.

In the United Kingdom, Imperial Chemical Industries converted the production methods at its Gloucester factory so as to give the operatives more responsibility for organizing their own activities and programming, and abolished the clocking-in system.

A project was introduced at Ferodo, manufacturers of brake linings, whereby operatives worked in groups of six, moving from one machine to another as required, having been trained to use all 14 machines in the group. Each team is responsible for its own workload and the workers see the visible results of their production at the end of the shift.

Dr Wilson concludes from these and other examples that

> It is usually possible to increase job satisfaction for most, though seldom all, members of a workforce, increase their learning, versatility and potential, greatly reduce absences (and in certain cases formal grievances) while increasing (or at least conserving) the productivity and feasibility of the enterprise.

The basic approach, he writes, is:

> To induce the worker to be less passively subordinate, more versatile and more self-directed . . . and to make all desirable work behaviour obviously rewarding through an appropriate combination of inherent and extrinsic rewards.

He warns, however, that there are numerous difficulties in preparing and organizing such schemes and that there must be the maximum advance planning and consultation.

The experiments are being closely watched by industrial planners and experts in Brussels. It was agreed at the Paris EEC summit to aim at a programme of 'job enrichment' throughout the Nine and the EEC Commissioner for Social Affairs, Dr Patrick Hillery, has placed it on an equal level of importance with workers' participation.

Although this development is still very much in its infancy, the question of job enrichment may come to have as revolutionary effect on industrial production and working conditions as did the Taylor scientific management principles in earlier days.

PART TWO

COUNTRY-BY-COUNTRY SURVEYS

5

Belgium

Economic Background

Belgium, with a population of just under 10 million and a land area of 30 500 square kilometres, has the second highest density in the EEC (318 inhabitants to the square km).

The capital, Brussels, has a population of 1.1 million. In the north, Antwerp (673 000) and Ghent (230 000) are the major cities, while Liège in the south-east has a population of 447 000. Population growth is relatively low.

There are linguistic and cultural differences between the north and south. The northerners (Flemings) are Dutch-speaking and account for over half the total population. The Walloons, in the south, speak French. Both languages are compulsory in schools. Brussels is officially bilingual. The northern areas (Flanders and Antwerp) are more highly industralized and have secured a major share of capital investment in modern growth industries. There has been constant friction between the two communities.

Brussels is the effective capital of the EEC.

Employment

About 3.7 million people are in gainful employment, of whom 2 million work in manufacturing. About one-third of the workers are women. Agriculture has declined to a point where it employs less than 5 per cent of the labour force. A growing proportion of the population is employed in service industries.

The most important industries are iron and steel, mechanical engineering, chemicals and petrochemicals and diamonds. Coalmining, once a staple industry, has steadily declined.

Unemployment has remained at about 2 per cent in recent years, a figure comparable to the European average.

There are about 600 000 immigrant workers, mainly from Italy and other Mediterranean countries.

Figure 5:1   Analysis of employment by principal sectors

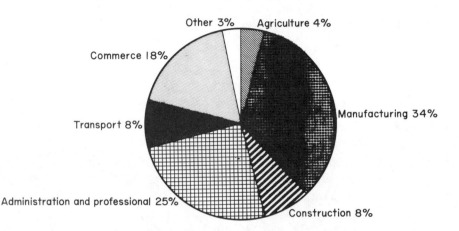

The Economy

Belgium had to cope with the problems arising from the need to restructure the economy following the loss of its colonies. The period between 1958 and 1965 was one of growth, followed by a mild recession and a revival starting in 1969. There was slower growth in 1971 and 1972 but the situation improved during 1973.

Foreign trade accounts for about 40 per cent of Belgium's GNP. France and West Germany together account for nearly 40 per cent of trade.

Government

Belgium is a constitutional monarchy, with a two-chamber parliament, the Senate and the Chamber of Deputies. Members of the Chamber are elected by universal suffrage on proportional representation.

Since the end of the Second World War, none of the three main parties — the Christian Social Party, Belgium Socialist and the Liberty and Progress (formerly Liberal) Party achieved an overall majority. The present government, formed in January 1973, under Socialist leader Edmund Leburton includes the Liberals.

Population density in principal regions

Number of inhabitants
per sq. km.

◻ 0 – 199

◼ 200 – 599

◼ 600+

Ostende

Brugge

FLAMANDE

Sint–Niklaas

Gent

Roeselare

Courtrai

Turnhout

Antwerpen

Mechelen

Diest

Hasselt

Brussels

BRUXELLES

•Tournai

Charleroi•

•Namur

•Liège

Verviers•

•Dinant

WALLONNE

Arlon•

Membership

The labour force in Belgium is more highly unionized than in any other
European country except Sweden. According to the latest available estimates
(end 1971) 67 per cent of the workers belong to unions out of a total
employed population of nearly 4 million. Apart from traditional and
historical reasons, the high membership can be attributed to practical factors.
Unions usually bargain to secure certain benefits exclusively for their own
members; they are also involved in administering social security, paying out
health and other benefits and thus making it more convenient for union
members to obtain these. In France, ideological divisions have acted as a
brake on recruitment, but in Belgium, growth has taken place despite the
pluralistic character of the movement.

The two main national centres are the Confederation of Christian Trade
Unions (CSC) which claims 1 million members and the Belgian Federation of
Labour (FGTB) with nearly 900 000. Less important is the Federation of
Liberal Unions (CGSLB) with about 135 000 members founded in 1930.
There are also a number of smaller specialist organizations.

The FGTB, founded in 1945, is the descendant of the original trade union
committee created in 1898 by the Belgian workers' party. It is Socialist in
outlook and has among its objectives the creation of 'a classless society'. The
Christian organization dates from 1908. Its constitution gives its aim as being
to realize 'a society based on Christian principles' (that is Catholic). The
Liberals believe in cooperation within the capitalist system. Both the
Christians and the Liberals support private enterprise.

All the centres are strongly linked with political parties and many
members of parliament belong to trade unions.

Figure 5:2 shows the growth of union membership during the postwar
years.

In certain types of industry, for example, metalworking, chemicals,
mining and petroleum, membership is as high as 90 per cent. It is less than
40 per cent among white-collar workers and non-existent among managerial
personnel.

The FGTB is strongest in such sectors as iron and steel, metal working,
transport, public services and in the larger companies.

The Christians predominate in the smaller plants and in food and
consumer goods industries. Although both are represented on joint industrial
committees and concerned with economic and social issues, there is no
evidence of any move towards unification. They have practical links on
wages and social conditions but their ideologies are poles apart.

Figure 5:2 Growth of union membership during postwar years in Belgium

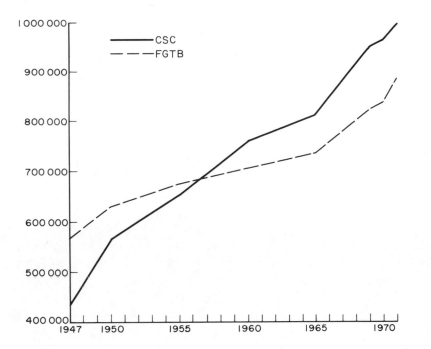

Attempts were made before the Second World War to form a single union centre, but they did not succeed.

Union organization is strongest in the central and coastal areas and weakest in the less developed provinces of Wallonia. In Eastern Flanders, the proportion of workers who are members of trade unions is estimated to be 97.5 per cent and in Western Flanders, 91.8 per cent, with 72 per cent in Antwerp and 75.8 per cent in Limbourg. In some of the provinces south of Brussels, such as Namur and Luxembourg, it is about 50 per cent and in Brabant, only 34 per cent.

The dispersal of membership of the main Christian unions (1971) was as follows:

Chemical and leather	45 367
Diamonds	7 032
Building and wood	175 869
Metal	174 819
Miners	31 662
Books and paper	16 425

Stone and cement	28 530
Textiles	121 890
Transport	11 829
Food	69 832
Salaried workers	117 713
Public service	62 732
Technical teachers	25 891
Railways and postal	38 009
Teaching	11 485

The strongest CSC sectors, numerically, are building, metal, textiles and salaried workers, all with over 100 000 members.

About 200 000 women belong to CSC unions..

Membership of the FGTB unions at the end of 1971 was:

General industrial	199 434
Salaried workers	106 132
Books and publishing	11 915
Diamonds	4 496
Journalists	157
Clothing	20 977
Entertainment	413
Metal	180 238
Miners	21 119
Public service	208 636
Textiles	49 317
Transport	25 606
Food	36 432

An additional 'centrale' covers young workers with about 23 000 members.

The relative influence of the two organizations can be gauged from a study of the votes cast for each in the elections to various works committees. In 1971, the Christians gained 47.61 per cent of the seats on works councils, and the Socialists 49.10. In the elections to the safety and health committees, the figures were: CSC, 51.49, FGTB 45.36. A regional analysis shows that in Wallonia the FGTB had 60.7 per cent of the seats on works councils compared with 37.3 per cent for the CSC, a slightly smaller majority in Brussels, but in Flemish areas, the Christians obtained 51.5 per cent of the seats compared with the FGTB's 34 per cent. The Christians were slightly more popular among salaried workers and young workers than the Socialists.

Structure

Belgian unions are not organized on a craft or occupational basis but are primarily industrial unions. They organize workers in the same industry or in closely related industries. The structure is highly centralized. Each national union has district branches in the regions, which have local sections in factories and enterprises, as well as local branches. Policy decisions are taken at the top, and wage negotiations tend to be on a national level.

The Socialists have 13 different industrial 'centrales' or centres and the Christians 18. All manual workers in an industry belong to the industrial union affiliated to the centre of their choice. It is therefore possible to find three different unions (ie Christian, Socialist, Liberal) functioning in the same plant.

The FGTB and CSC hold delegate congresses and in each day-to-day control is exercised by an executive committee or bureau. As well as the industrial (horizontal) organization, there are regional federations which group together the various industrial 'centrales' on a local basis.

At factory level, there are usually union delegations (délégations syndicales), who may be elected or appointed by regional union officials. Their number depends on the size of the enterprise and there are generally separate delegations for manual and non-manual workers. The employer is not legally obliged to recognize them, but usually does so under union pressure. The first collective agreement on delegations was reached in 1947 at national level and was followed by similar agreements in about 40 industries. In 1971 a further agreement provided that, on request from any of the workers' organizations, an employer should agree to the setting up of a delegation.

A delegate's job is similar to that of a shop steward. He deals with grievances and checks the application of collective agreements on wages and working conditions. He has security of employment, since he may not be dismissed on account of his union activities.

All Belgian unions provide extensive social and welfare benefits. Union contributions vary in different groups in the FGTB (50 francs to 200 francs per month) and in the CSC the rate was raised from 132 francs in January 1970 to 157 francs in January 1973.

Collective Bargaining and Industrial Relations

The system of industrial relations in Belgium is based on the concept of 'the most representative trade union organization'. The three organizations – Socialist, Christian and Liberal – are recognized as 'most representative' by the government and the employers' associations, but in practice they recognize the Socialist and the Christian bodies. The three organizations represent the interests of the workers at national, industrial and factory levels and only they have the right to conclude legally binding collective agreements. An Act of 1968 laid down four criteria for the 'representativeness' of workers' central organizations:

1   They must have an 'inter-occupational' character.
2   They must be established at national level.
3   They must be represented on the Central Economic Council and the National Labour Council.
4   They must have at least 50 000 members.

The same criteria (apart from that of membership) normally apply to employers' organizations. The most important of these is the Federation of Belgian Enterprises. This comprises 48 associations including foreign-owned companies.

The object of the 1968 Act was to establish firmly the principle of industry-wide bargaining and standardize negotiating practice.

Responsibility for collective bargaining lies with joint industrial committees (commissions paritaires) of employer and worker representatives. There are 83 such committees and they are the cornerstone of collective bargaining procedures. They are established by Royal Order and generally cover an entire sector of an industry, appointing subcommittees, where necessary, to operate in a more limited field. They have an independent chairman and vice-chairman. Their main functions are: to make collective agreements, to provide conciliation for preventing or settling disputes, and to give advice on relevant matters to the various official bodies.

If a committee or one of its organizations so requests, the Minister of Labour may issue an order extending the scope of the agreement or take action to make it binding.

The emphasis on national bargaining does not rule out the practice of plant bargaining. The national agreement sets minima and these are usually improved through local negotiations. In the chemical industry most of the bargaining is carried on at plant level, though in metalworking, employers and unions are anxious to maintain the supremacy of national agreements. Plant negotiations are usually conducted by union officials, in consultation with the factory delegates, who often have the final say in settling a figure.

Since 1960, collective bargaining has been based on the principle of 'social programming'. This term has never been clearly defined, but its general object is to avoid industrial conflict and enable workers to share in national prosperity. A three-point agreement reached between unions and employers' associations in 1963 laid down:

1   Workers should enjoy a regularly improving standard of living through economic expansion.
2   This objective should be attained through national industrial collective agreements, determining the workers' share in the growth of the national economy during a given period.
3   Industrial peace should be observed during the currency of a collective agreement.

Social programming also covers such matters as family allowances, paid holidays, manpower policy, hours of work, pensions, the activities of works councils, guaranteed incomes for manual workers and the revision of collective agreements.

Most collective agreements last for two years (for example, in metal-working, petroleum, textiles and building) and there has been some pressure from the rank and file to get the period reduced. Many contain a specific 'no-strike' clause in which unions undertake to refrain from industrial action during the period of an agreement. Some contain a provision that only union members can receive such benefits as productivity bonuses, supplementary unemployment and pension benefits. Nearly all make provision for conciliation and arbitration operating through a subcommittee of the joint industry machinery. There is no compulsory arbitration but the government will intervene in disputes affecting public welfare.

Because of the effective joint industrial machinery and the centralized character of union organizations, Belgium has been relatively strike free. Workers have the right to strike, but union leaders tend to regard the strike weapon as a last resort.

They thus have in effect the task of 'policing' their members to secure the observance of the no-strike clause. Strike pay may be withheld from unofficial strikers. Unions receive a subsidy from employers, amounting to 0.6 per cent of gross wages, in return for safeguarding social peace. But the subsidy is reduced if a union supports strikers.

During 1970 there was a series of unofficial strikes at plant level in breach of no-strike clauses. This was attributed to workers' growing impatience at the lengthy period of the contract and some lack of contact between union officials and their rank and file.

Actual figures of days lost through strikes in Belgium are shown in Figure 5:3.

Figure 5:3   Industrial disputes in Belgium

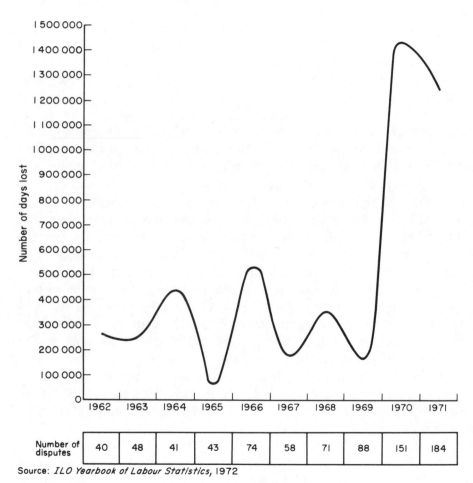

Number of disputes	40	48	41	43	74	58	71	88	151	184

Source: *ILO Yearbook of Labour Statistics,* 1972

The Balance Sheet

As a result of strong and centralized trade unions and the adoption of 'social programming', workers in Belgium have enjoyed a rapidly rising standard of living (Figure 5:4), although as elsewhere in Europe, the gains have been eroded by rising prices (Figure 5:5). Nevertheless, real wages increased by 56 per cent between 1958 and 1970.

Figure 5:4   Wages (1966 = 100)

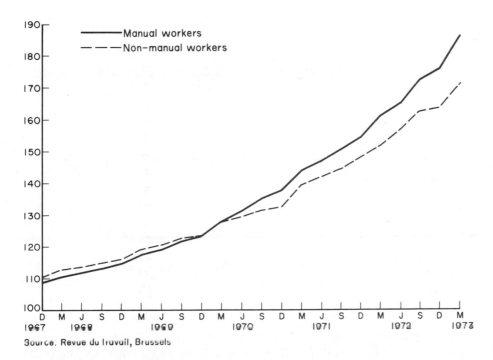

Source. Revue du Travail, Brussels

Hours are being progressively reduced and the aim is to bring them down from 42 in 1972-3 to 40 in 1975-6. Holiday entitlement is 3 weeks plus 10 public holidays. The unions have been pressing for an extra week's paid leave.

Belgium has a comprehensive system of social security, the employer bearing 50 per cent of the cost. Contributions and benefits are related to income and linked with the cost of living index.

Figure 5:5   Consumer prices

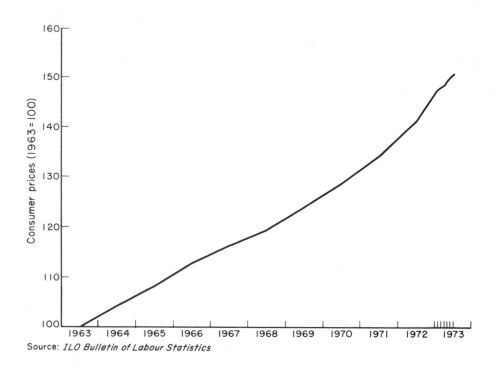

Source: *ILO Bulletin of Labour Statistics*

Cooperation

Under a law of 1948, as subsequently amended, an employer is obliged to set up a works council (conseil d'entreprise) if he employs more than 150 workers. Each council consists of workers' and managerial representatives in varying proportions but the employer's side may not have more than the workers'. The head of the concern, or his representative acts as chairman. Worker members are elected from lists of candidates nominated by the trade unions, while those on management side are chosen by the employer. Elections are held every four years and all workers vote, whether or not they belong to a union. There are no separate councils for non-manual workers.

The councils are advisory. Members can express their views on the organization of the firm, working rules and conditions, productivity, engagement and dismissal, social welfare and all subjects affecting their interests. The employer alone has the right of decision-making in economic matters. Managements are obliged to keep the councils informed about the firm's financial position and future plans. When such information is not divulged the workers can take the employer to court and they have the right to ask an auditor to check the information given by the employer. Council members are protected against dismissal.

There are also compulsory committees on safety and health in all factories with more than 50 workers.

The Christian and Socialist unions are, broadly, equally represented on the various committees.

In the opinion of some Belgian authorities on labour relations, the powers of works councils have not been sufficiently clearly or precisely defined, and financial and economic information is not always provided – or understood. Belgian unions aim to train worker members to acquire a better understanding of economic subjects. They also seek the introduction of compulsory and uniform rules regarding company auditors.

Belgian workers have less say in the management of the enterprise for which they work than their opposite numbers in Germany.

Nationally, however, there is ample machinery for joint employer-union cooperation and the general climate of industrial relations is favourable.

During the Second World War employers and union leaders met secretly to work out a blue print for their future relations and for social reform, covering practically every aspect of industrial activity. This tradition has survived. The 'social partners' as the two sides call themselves, agree on broad general terms and they have established a tradition of mutual confidence and a sound working relationship on a pragmatic basis without elaborate legislation. Trade unions in Belgium do not have any legal personality – a somewhat astonishing omission – and they cannot be sued for breach of agreements.

Apart from the joint industrial committees (commission paritaires), employers and unions come together centrally on the National Labour Council. There are in all 22 representatives, under an independent chairman. The Council's main function is to advise the nation's administrators on labour and social matters and to arbitrate where joint committees fail to reach agreement. Since the 1968 Act it has been empowered to conclude national agreements. These have been reached in matters affecting employment, income security and the functions of works councils. It has been described (*ILO Review*) as 'a kind of social parliament enacting general rules that apply to the whole private sector of the economy'. The government listens to, but in no way interferes with the activities of the Council.

The government does, however, play a direct role in labour relations and collective bargaining in the public sector, where the same kind of machinery for works councils and workers' delegations exists as in private enterprise.

There are many other joint advisory bodies, for example the Central economic council, the Office for the increase of productivity, the Bureau of economic programming and the National committee for economic expansion. In these ways, the two sides of industry succeed in making their influence felt on the government's policy-makers.

6

Denmark

Economic Background

Denmark's population reached 5 million during 1972. Its total land area is just under 43 000 square kilometres, half of which is formed by the peninsula of Jutland. The rest consists of about 500 islands, 100 of which are inhabited. Excluding Greenland and the Faeroe Islands, which are part of Denmark, the density of population is 114 per square km.

Copenhagen, the capital, is situated on Zealand, the largest island. The Greater Copenhagen area, with a population of 1.4 million, accounts for over one quarter of the country's total population.

Major towns on the mainland are Aarhus, Aalborg, Esbjerg; Odense the capital of Funen has a population of 133 000.

Employment

Though Denmark is still regarded primarily as an agricultural country, the farming sector employs only 11 per cent of the labour force. The decline in agriculture is due to the shift in the late 1940s to industry when industrial exports began to surpass agricultural sales. The total labour force is about 2½ million, with about 680 000 in manufacturing industry and a well developed services sector.

Denmark has no indigenous raw materials and imports steel, fuel and other materials. Among its more important industries are shipbuilding, engineering, chemicals, textiles, furniture, glass and foods.

Unemployment has remained low, but the country experienced a rise in unemployment in the early 1970s, reaching 3.8 per cent of the insured

Figure 6:1 Analysis of employment by principal sectors

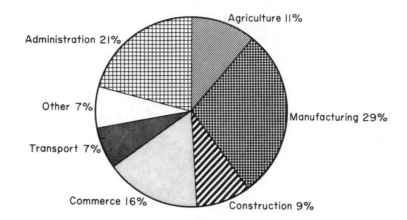

population in 1971.

The Economy

Denmark's GNP was £7,220 million (1971). The economy grew rapidly during the 1960s when there was an average growth rate of 4.9 per cent per annum. Growth rates were 3.7 per cent and 4 per cent in 1970 and 1972 respectively, and about 5½ per cent in 1973.

Foreign trade accounts for one third of Denmark's GNP. Industrial exports are responsible for 65 per cent of the total and agricultural exports for 20 per cent. The principal markets for Danish goods are the UK, Sweden and West Germany, and the main exports consist of industrial raw materials, food and consumer goods.

Government

Denmark is a constitutional monarchy, with a one-chamber parliament (Folketing) elected by universal suffrage. The head of state is the monarch, who appoints the Prime Minister, but has no political power.

Since the end of the Second World War, Denmark has been governed by Social-democratic governments or coalitions dominated by the Social-democrats. Between 1968 and 1971 a centre-right coalition was formed between Conservatives, Radicals and Liberals, but a new coalition between the Social-democrats and the left-wing People's Party took over in 1971, with an effective majority of one seat.

The Prime Minister since October 1972 has been Anker Jørgensen, former chairman of the General Workers' Union, Denmark's largest union. He was succeeded in December 1973 by Poul Hartling when the Liberal-democratic party took over after a general election.

Population density in principal regions

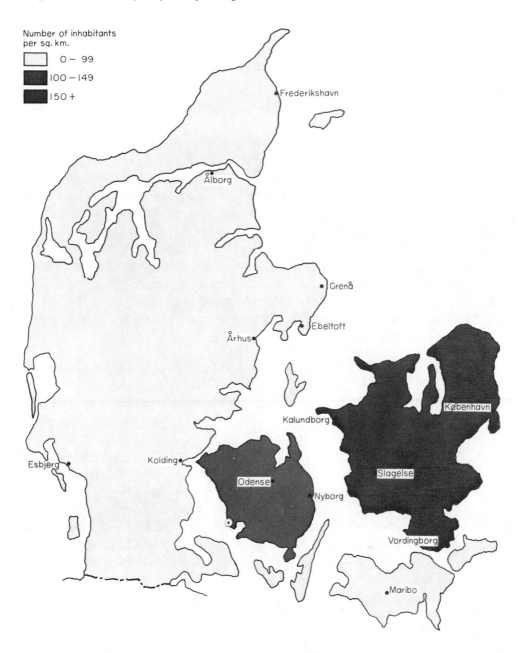

Number of inhabitants
per sq. km.

☐ 0 – 99
■ 100 – 149
■ 150 +

Frederikshavn

Ålborg

Grenå

Ebeltoft

Århus

Kalundborg

Kolding

Esbjerg

Odense

Nyborg

Slagelse

København

Vordingborg

Maribo

Membership and Structure

A high proportion — 65-70 per cent — of Denmark's workers belong to trade unions. Nearly all unions are affiliated to the powerful Federation of Danish Trade Unions — Landsorganisationen i Danmark, LO — which has over 920 000 members. There is a separate Federation of Civil Servants and Salaried Employees (FTF) covering about 14 per cent of trade union members but the majority of white-collar workers belong to LO unions. A further 3 per cent belong to a council (FAF) which looks after the interests of supervisors and technical employees in private industry.

LO was founded in 1898 and brought together the various organizations which had been springing up since the 1870s. It originally comprised 38 national unions and 25 local organizations with a total of 60 000 members. The first years were turbulent and there were violent clashes betwen the two sides of industry. A lock-out in 1899 lasted for three months and involved 40 000 workers. It ended with the 'September Agreement' which set the pattern for employer-worker relationships which still exists. The agreement was modernized in 1960.

There are no divisions on political or religious lines.

Membership grew rapidly, as shown below:

1900	96 000
1910	123 000
1920	355 000
1930	339 000
1940	543 000
1950	714 000
1960	776 000
1970	896 000
1972	909 500

By the beginning of January 1973 there were 924 178 members. LO estimates that about 95 per cent of Denmark's industrial workers are organized, compared with 60-65 per cent in the non-manual field. About a quarter of the members are women.

LO is a centralized body. Workers are organized according to their occupation or trade, and the central organization comprises 49 national unions, with 133 local (geographical) federations and about 2000 individual occupational unions. There has been a marked tendency towards mergers. Whereas there were 64 unions in 1966, the number had fallen to 49 in 1973.

The biggest union covers general workers, with nearly 260 000 members. The metalworkers have 100 000 members and the commercial and clerical union 118 000. Most of the other unions (railwaymen, postmen, textile workers, garment workers, electricians and printers) range from 10 000 to 20 000 members. The trend towards amalgamation has been accelerating. The Danish movement is based on national and local unions. The basic unit at the workplace is the union 'club'. If several workers in different crafts are employed at the same place, they may form a joint club. Geographically, the basic unit is the branch, which comprises all workers in the same category within a town or locality. They vary in size and influence. Some are directly represented in negotiations and play a part in ensuring that agreed wages and conditions are applied. In larger towns, there are trades councils.

Nationally, all unions cover the workers in a particular trade or industry. They hold congresses – usually every 3 to 5 years – at which the leaders are elected. There are also 'cartel' organizations, which cover a multiplicity of unions in the same industry, for example building and engineering.

Trade unions have many functions in the field of social welfare, for example they are responsible for the administration of unemployment insurance.

Shop stewards are recognized and function in most workplaces. They are protected against arbitrary dismissal.

The LO

The congress which meets every 4 years, and is attended by about 1000 delegates, is the supreme authority of LO. It alone can amend or change the constitution, and its decisions are binding on the general council and the executive committee. The executive committee is elected by congress and consists of a president, vice-president, treasurer and 16 members. It can also include the representatives of the Social-democrat party. The general council consists of the executive committee, plus representatives of affiliated organizations, on the basis of 1 per 2000 members or fraction thereof. The council meets at least once a year, or more often if necessary.

LO's philosophy is social democratic. According to its constitution, its object is to 'unite national unions in order to ensure the protection of the workers' interests and to work for the achievement of industrial and economic democracy'.

Among its functions, LO is required:

1   To assist affiliated organizations, particularly where employers attempt

to oppose union activity or impede efforts to improve working conditions.

2   To promote unity of action among its affiliated organizations.

3   To give advice and guidance on union problems and labour legislation,
     and help unions present their cases before the Labour Court.

4   To disseminate information about the tasks and objects of the movement
     among union members and the general public.

5   To maintain international relations with other free unions.

6   To research into economic and social matters and encourage union
     education and publicity.

7   To help settle inter-union disputes and encourage mutual assistance in
     the case of strikes or lock-outs.

8   To support all democratic organizations, such as the Cooperative move-
     ment and, in cooperation with the Social-democrat party, promote
     legislation designed to further the interests of the workers.

In accordance with its objects, the LO carries on an intensive and efficient
programme of education and information. There is a special association for
workers' education and training, with institutes at Esbjerg, Roskilde and
Elsinore, attended by trade unionists from every branch of industry.

LO publishes a journal and issues regular information bulletins about
wages and economic conditions which act as a guide to unions in their
negotiations. Many individual unions run their own educational and propaganda schemes.

There is nothing very revolutionary about the LO programme, nor about
the declaration which was adopted at its congress in 1971. In this, the main
emphasis was on the need to 'democratize' economic institutions and provide
opportunities for workers to share in capital formation and in the management of companies.

The LO's opposite number on the employers' side is the Danish Employers Confederation (DA) founded in 1896. It is a federation of employers'
associations on an industrial and regional basis, as well as including individual
firms. It comprises 225 member organizations and 290 member firms,
employing about 400 000 manual and over 100 000 office workers. There
are ten industrial federations and members are grouped in 68 local federations. The central authority is the general assembly which elects a central
council of 54 members. This council elects a president, vice-president and
executive committee of 15, which appoints a board of directors to run the
DA's day-to-day affairs.

The DA exercises a stricter authority over its constituents than exists in any EEC country. Individual employers may not enter into collective bargains on wage rates, hours, holidays and other forms of remuneration without the prior agreement of the general council. Failure to reach agreement must be immediately reported to the DA.

Collective Bargaining and Industrial Relations

Collective bargaining is not only customary in Denmark but is legally required. The general procedures are laid down in the 'Main' agreement of 1960, which replaced the original 'September' agreement of 1899.

The agreement covers the following principal points:

1   Recognition of the rights of free association.
2   Rules about strikes and lock-outs during the currency of a collective agreement.
3   Provision for honouring agreements.
4   Respect for the employer's right to 'direct and distribute' work, with safeguards against arbitrary dismissal.
5   Exemption, if required, from union membership of supervisors, foremen and other employers' representatives.
6   Rules for the termination of agreements.
7   Where practicable, the inclusion of shop steward rules in collective agreements.
8   An undertaking 'to promote cooperation . . . and work for peaceful and stable working conditions in the enterprises through joint consultation committees or other suitable bodies'.
9   Encouragement for the adoption of wage systems designed to increase productivity.
10 The Main agreement to remain in force unless denounced by either party giving six months notice.

The agreement was signed by 8 representatives each of the DA and the LO.

The general pattern of wage settlements is set at national level between the central organizations and is followed by negotiations at industry level. It is possible to have direct bargaining at company level, where improvements on the national rate are secured. Collective bargaining covers wages, hours, holidays, job security, redundancy and dismissal, pensions and other aspects of social welfare.

Collective contracts are normally due to expire at the same date. They usually last for a two-year period, after intensive bargaining between the parties in the late autumn; adjustments are made at six-monthly intervals in the light of movements in the cost of living index. The period of notice to terminàte agreements is three months. If an agreement has been denounced, or has expired, its provisions will continue to apply until a new agreement has been reached.

Mediation plays an important part in Danish industrial relations. There is a state conciliation board which can offer its services to either side and its suggestions for a settlement are put to a secret ballot vote. The Board, which functions under the Conciliation in Labour Disputes Act 1958, amended 1961, consists of 3 members appointed by the Minister of Labour. Conciliators are empowered to postpone a threatened stoppage if they consider it will impede the prospects of a peaceful settlement.

As elsewhere in Scandinavia, two types of conflict are distinguished — conflicts of interest and conflicts of right. The former are dealt with through mediation; the latter, which concern the interpretation or violation of agreements, may be referred to an industrial arbitration board or to the Labour Court, if direct negotiations break down. The Court, originally created in 1919 under an Act amended by subsequent legislation, consists of 6 members, 16 substitute members, a president, 3 vice-presidents and a secretary. The procedure before the Court is the same as that in ordinary courts. Its decisions are final and binding. In fact, most conflicts of right are resolved in preliminary negotiations and few reach the Court.

Disputes

Once an agreement has been entered into, both parties are obliged to preserve the peace for the period of the agreement. A stoppage is legally permissible on the renewal of an agreement, but it must be approved by a three-quarters majority. At least 14 days notice must be given as a first warning and 7 days as a second warning. Workers are obliged to go through all the machinery for peaceful settlement before striking.

The result of this procedural machinery is that strikes have been infrequent in Denmark (see Figure 6:2). Between 1961 and 1970 an average of 414 working days per year for 1000 workers was lost in disputes. It would have been lower but for major stoppages in 1961 and 1970. Very few working days were lost in 1971, but in the spring of 1973 Denmark experienced its biggest strike on record. This involved nearly 260 000 trade unionists — 150 000 on strike and 110 000 locked-out — cost 3.5 million working days and lasted for 3 weeks. The dispute, which was over the new

Figure 6:2   Industrial disputes in Denmark

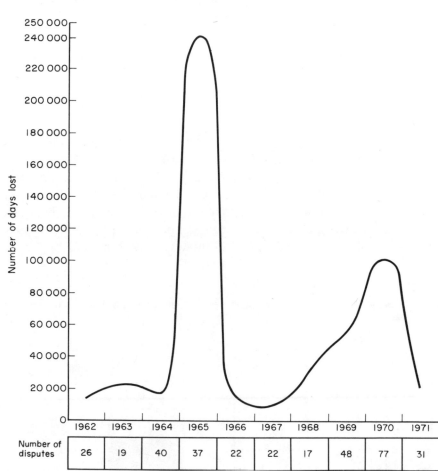

Number of disputes	26	19	40	37	22	22	17	48	77	31

Source: *ILO Yearbook of Labour Statistics*, 1972

pay agreement, was settled on a compromise basis – equal pay for men and women, the introduction of a 40-hour week as from December 1974, an extra week's holiday for shift workers, staged increase in the basic wage and improved arrangements for cost of living adjustments and the establishment of works educational funds. It was expected to lead to increases of about 9 per cent a year plus a wage drift of 5 per cent.

The settlement was reached after the intervention of the state conciliators. Over two-thirds of the workers and four-fifths of the employers voted in favour in the ballot.

The Balance Sheet

Danish workers have enjoyed a progressively rising standard of living. Like other Scandinavian countries, Denmark has always been noted for social reform, and, in term of food consumption, education, housing and social security, it is one of the most advanced in West Europe. Much of the advance can be attributed to the existence of strong trade unions and their tradition of cooperation.

Wage levels are among the highest in the EEC and have continued to rise rapidly. Money incomes rose by 10 per cent in 1971, compared with 13 per cent in the two preceding years (OECD). Hourly earnings of non-agricultural workers which had risen by about 11 per cent a year during the second half of the 1960s increased by 15 per cent between 1970 and 1971 – the largest postwar increase experienced. The movement in hourly earnings between 1969 and 1971 is shown in Figure 6:3. It was expected that hourly earnings would increase by about 11 per cent (including wage drift) in 1972.

Figure 6:3   Percentage increase in hourly earnings between 1969 and 1971

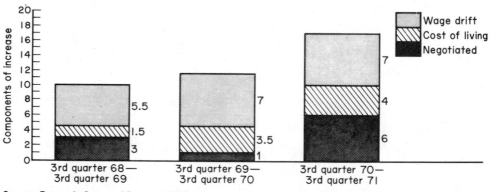

Source: Economic Survey of Denmark 1972

A fairly strict system of price control is operated under the Prices and Profits Act, but even so, non-agricultural prices rose relatively rapidly during the early years of the 1970s – 6-7 per cent in 1970 and 5-6 per cent in 1971. The monthly price index (excluding housing) stood at 150 and the end of 1971 compared with 134 at the beginning of 1970 (January 1963 – 100).

The working week is to be reduced from 41¾ hours to 40 as a result of the 1973 strike settlement. There are 18 days paid holiday with 10 public holidays.

The Danes enjoy very generous benefits in the form of sickness, disablement, old age and other types of social insurance, as well as family allowances. The state provides subsidies for housing, education, health and food. About 60 per cent of the cost of the National Health Service and social security is borne by the government. Most benefits are related to earnings. In addition to the flat-rate state pension scheme, there is a supplementary labour market (ATP) scheme, introduced in 1964, which applies to all wage-earners between 18 and 66. One-third of the contributions are paid by the worker, two-thirds by the employer and the system is administered by a joint employer-union board, under an independent chairman.

Cooperation

Danish trade unionists, like those in Sweden, are not in favour of extending public ownership as a means of achieving their aim of greater economic equality. Instead, they rely on increasing the national wealth and then securing a bigger share in it for the workers. This is the objective of a Bill designed to promote economic democracy, originally due to enter into force on 1 July 1973, but postponed because of the March-April strike. Its main points are designed to give wage-earners a substantial share in the ownership of the private sector, in capital accumulation and in the running of their concern, and to encourage savings and redistribute wealth. The Bill was worked out with full trade union support, indeed the impetus for it came from the metalworkers, but the employers' associations and the opposition parties were opposed to it.

The employers' confederation argued in a memorandum on the Bill that 'the formation of a huge investment under the majority control of the trade unions and a new centralized bureaucracy is deemed to create the opposite of a "near democracy". The road to forced socialization opened up by the Bill seems unavoidably to be made even wider'. It described the Bill as 'the most controversial issue' for decades and stated that it would lead to a worsening of relations between industry and government and adversely affect the national economy.

The main proposal is the establishment of a comprehensive 'dividend and investment fund', financed by employers' contributions, collectively owned by employees and managed by a council consisting of 60 (36 union and 24 government nominees) under the supervision of a parliamentary board.

All employers, including those in the public sector, would contribute through a levy on their payroll of half per cent in the first year, rising by half a percentage point per year until 1983, when it reaches 5 per cent a year.

Wage-earners would receive a certificate each year and a dividend. Shares would be redeemable after a minimum of 5 years at their market value. Assets paid to the fund would be invested over a wide field, including land, property, mortgage bonds and shares. According to union estimates, the fund would in 20 years' time account for over a quarter of all business investment and would have total assets of £500 million within 5 years.

In all companies of over 50 employees, two worker members would be appointed to the board. Wage-earners would be represented by their own elected representatives at company general meetings.

Among the advantages seen for the scheme by the trade unions are that it is universal and egalitarian; it combines an investment fund with dividend sharing and gains for the workers a share in the business as well as a voice in decision-making. The employers' main objection is that it constitutes a form of pay-roll tax, which will increase costs and undermine investment and competitiveness.

Before the Bill comes into effect, there will be a period of intensive discussion and argument throughout the country.

The proposed economic democracy scheme is additional to the existing system of works councils or 'cooperation committees' which were set up by voluntary agreement in October 1970. Before then, there were agreements on joint consultative committees.

By 1971 there were 705 cooperation committees. The agreement recognized the workers' right to codetermination (shared responsibility) in matters involving workshop and factory organization, safety, welfare and personnel policy. It identified another sphere of 'coinfluence' which provided the opportunity for workers' representatives to exchange ideas and make suggestions to influence management policy decisions. The committees receive information about their company's financial situation and prospects. They consist of equal number of management and workers' representatives and there is a central Joint Cooperation Board which regularly checks progress and encourages participation.

Nationally, employers and union leaders meet together on the Labour Market Council which is a forum for discussion on employment and industrial relations. The Council meets under the chairmanship of the permanent secretary of the Ministry of Labour.

Both sides are regularly consulted by the government on all aspects of labour and social legislation, but relations, as might be expected, are particularly close with the trade unions.

The Danish government backs voluntary management-labour agreements with legislation to give them force. There is a network of social and labour laws covering not only social security and welfare, but such matters as dismissals, apprenticeship, employment of women and minors, and salary during sickness and military service.

The strength of the system, however, resides in the tradition of voluntary cooperation between national leaders of the two sides of industry, and the degree of authority exercised by the central organizations and the self-discipline of the Danish workers.

7

France

Economic Background

France is the largest country in Europe, with an area of 544 000 square kilometres. Its total population is just over 51 million, the fourth largest in the EEC, after West Germany, the United Kingdom and Italy. Its density of population at 93 persons per square km is lower only in the Republic of Ireland.

The principal concentration of population is in the Paris basin. Paris, the capital, has a population of 2 607 000 inhabitants, while the population of Greater Paris which includes the surrounding metropolitan area, is 8 197 000. The only other cities with populations of over 500 000 are Marseille (894 000) and Lyon (535 000). Other major cities include Toulouse (371 000) Nice (322 000) Bordeaux (267 000) Nantes (259 000) Strasbourg (249 000) and Lille (191 000).

Population growth has been rapid since the end of the Second World War, as a result of declining mortality and increasing birth rates, as well as of large-scale immigration

Employment

The French labour force totals about 20 million, of whom 5.5 million work in manufacturing and 3 million in agriculture. Unemployment has remained at a low level and manpower shortages have been made good by importing foreign labour.

Apart from Italy, France is the most agriculture-oriented member of the EEC. Agriculture employs just under 15 per cent of the work force, and much of industry is engaged in the preparation and processing of food and wines. Though considerable advances have been made in production techniques, much of the agricultural sector is relatively backward, and most farms operate on a small scale.

Industry has expanded rapidly since 1945, with the emphasis·on modern technological industries, such as ˙electrical engineering and electronics, and petrochemicals. Traditional industries, such as coalmining, have declined, partly as the result of the switch to new sources of energy, for example, natural gas. The government offers incentives to encourage companies to settle in the less-developed areas. Advice and financial assistance to firms are available from the Institut de Developpement Industriel (IDI) which is concerned with the study of problems in traditional and modern sectors.

Figure 7:1   Analysis of employment by principal sectors

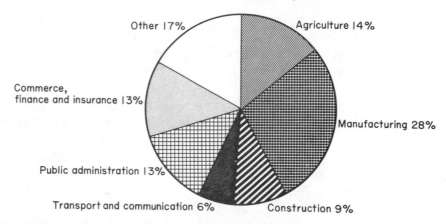

The Economy

The French economy achieved a remarkable rate of growth during the 1960s, a rate which was higher than in any other member of the EEC. Between 1965 and 1970, the GNP achieved a volume growth of 5.5 per cent per annum, reaching £72 500 million in 1970. The problems caused by the industrial unrest of May 1968 were overcome by devaluation of the franc, strict credit restrictions and budgetary control, but inflation has remained a serious problem in France.

Trade accounts for about 17 per cent of France's gross domestic product. There has been a considerable shift towards trade with other European

Population density in principal regions

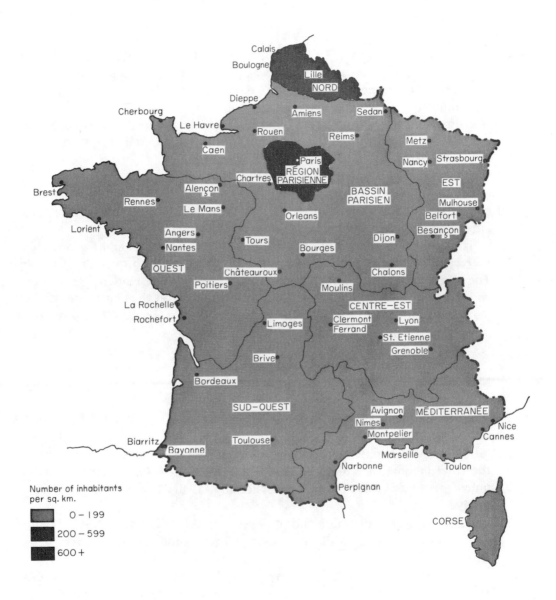

Number of inhabitants
per sq. km.

0 – 199

200 – 599

600 +

countries, the members of the original Six accounting for about half the volume of both imports and exports.

Government

France became a republic in 1870. In the period between the two world wars until 1958, when General de Gaulle assumed power, there were few periods of stable government. Since that date, the Gaullists have held office continuously. The social and industrial unrest of May 1968 came near to overthrowing the government, but the Gaullists retained the initiative and introduced strict measures of economic reform. General de Gaulle retired in 1969 and was succeeded by M Georges Pompidou.

The President, elected for a period of 7 years, holds executive power and appoints a Council of Ministers, headed by the Prime Minister. Parliament is composed of two Chambers — the National Assembly and the Senate, the latter being elected on a regional basis.

There are two major left-wing parties, the Communists and the Socialists. In recent elections, they have formed electoral pacts to oust the Gaullists. The most important of the centre groups are the Independent Republicans and the Centre for Progress and Reform. Though both the centre and the left parties made gains in the 1973 elections, the Gaullists succeeded in retaining power, with M Pierre Messmer as Prime Minister.

Membership

The development of trade unionism in France has not matched the nation's industrial and economic growth. Precise figures are not available, but it is estimated that union membership represents only about 20-25 per cent of the total labour force of 15 million. The influence of the unions is, however, much greater, politically and professionally, than their membership would imply.

The low degree of unionization arises from historical and political factors and a brief historical outline is necessary for an understanding of the present situation.

The trade union movement developed later than in Britain and although the first unions were established in the 1860s among craft workers, it was not until 1884 that they obtained legal recognition. The Confédération générale du travail was set up as a national centre in 1895, nearly thirty years after the establishment of the British TUC.

Even at that date, the CGT adopted ostensibly revolutionary policies. Its first general secretary wrote:

> Social justice can result only from the expropriation of the capitalists and the setting up of an equalitarian society in which production and distribution are organized by the trade unions.

The revolutionary ideals were succeeded on the outbreak of the First World War by a wave of patriotism and nationalistic fervour which lasted until revulsion against the war coincided with the Russian Revolution. From then onwards began a period of schism and strife which has characterized the movement down the years. Within the CGT itself there were those who disagreed with Communist doctrines and wanted to achieve social progress through evolution rather than revolution. The first break-away was that of a group of Catholics who formed the Confédération française des travailleurs chrétiens (CFTC) in 1919, with the main object of promoting 'peaceful collaboration between capital and labour'. The CGT itself split over the Russian issue and the foundation of the Communist International. In 1921 the Communists formed their independent 'CGT unitaire', leaving the main body of the CGT in the hands of moderate leaders, like Léon Jouhaux, who practised international cooperation and played a major part in building up the International Labour Organization.

The two wings of the CGT were reunited at the time of the Popular Front government in 1936, but the Communists were expelled after the signature of the Soviet-German pact in 1939. They were readmitted after the German invasion of the USSR and the Nazi occupation of France and carried on a joint struggle against the occupying forces. When the war ended, the Communists were found to be the majority section within the CGT. They have dominated it ever since.

The outbreak of the Cold War and the split inside the international trade union movement were paralleled by a new schism within the CGT. The Socialist section 'Force ouvrière' (named after the journal of the Socialist section — the Communist equivalent is 'Vie ouvrière') broke away in December 1947, following a Communist-inspired strike wave. The CGT-FO never attained the same influence among the mass of French industrial workers as the CGT.

The next important development was the transformation of the Christian confederation into the Confédération française démocratique du travail (CFDT) in 1964. This body grew from acceptance of the view that the Christian ethic was no longer suitable as a basis for action. It adopted a policy of extreme left-wing democratic socialism. The Christian confederation remained in being with a much depleted membership.

The membership of the various bodies is estimated to be:

CGT: about 2 million members
CFDT: about 6-700 000
CGT-FO: about 500 000
CFTC: about 150 000

(At the end of the Second World War the CGT claimed 5½ million members and the CFTC 350 000.)

A different organization, the Confédération générale des cadres (CGC) caters for executives, foremen, technicians and salesmen. It has about 210 000 members, but many executives belong to unions within the main confédérations.

Teachers have their separate autonomous organization, the Fedération de l'éducation nationale (FEN), in which the Force ouvrière type of policy is dominant. About 90 per cent of teachers are organized.

There are also a number of 'independent' or 'autonomous' organizations, usually linked with a single industry or company, and mainly to be found in the Paris area. The main bodies are the Confédération générale des syndicats (CGSI), the Confédération française du travail (CFT) and the Confédération autonome du travail (CAT).

The strength and influence of these organizations is however very limited. Finally, there is the small Confédération nationale du travail (CNT) which is a relic of the anarcho-syndicalist traditions of the early days of the CGT.

Thus, leaving aside the independent organizations and the separate teachers' organization, there are three main national confederations to be reckoned with. This fragmentation on political and ideological lines is probably one of the main reasons for the low membership of French trade unions. Membership of a trade union has not the same emotive value as in Britain, and the absence of anything like 'closed' or 'union' shops (except in the docks and certain sections of printing) removes any pressure on individual workers to join.

Since any worker has the right to belong to the union of his choice, one finds members of the CGT, the Force ouvrière and the CFDT working alongside one another in the same plant. Common action at plant level is a recognition of the realities of the situation.

Workers are highly organized in the public sector, particularly the gas and electricity and railway industries. Organization is weak in retail trade, building, textiles and consumer goods industries, though it has developed strongly in the modern industries such as electronics, oil and chemicals. The CGT membership is strongest in the public sector and in such plants as the Renault car enterprise. Geographically the CGT is strongest in the industrial areas of the north, Paris, the southeast, the centre and the exteme west of Britanny.

Figure 7:2   Support for unions in elections to workers councils

	Per cent support First collège	Per cent support Second collège	Total
CGT	53.9	16.5	46.0
CFDT	20.2	17.5	19.6
CGT-FO	7.4	7.2	7.3
CFTC	2.6	3.3	2.7
CGC	—	25.8	5.5
Others	5.9	11.2	7.0
Non-union	10.0	18.5	11.9

An idea of the relative support for each of the main organizations can be gained from the results of the elections to the works councils, which are organized in every enterprise. These are divided into two 'collèges' (electoral colleges), one for manual and clerical workers and the other for technicians, foremen and other executive grades. The most recent figures available give the breakdown shown in Figure 7:2.

This analysis underlines the predominance of the CGT among manual workers and its relative weakness among technicians and supervisors. It also shows the relatively poor degree of support for the Force ouvrière and the Christian confederation and places the CFDT second in importance.

It is not possible to obtain reliable statistics about industry-by-industry membership. Trade union accounting is not very systematic. The procedure is that stamps are distributed from a central point and local secretaries or treasurers endeavour to sell them month by month. There may thus be a large number of union members holding union cards, which are not fully stamped up.

Structure

Despite their ideological differences, there is considerable similarity in the structure and machinery of the three main confederations (CGT, CGT-FO, CFDT). All are based on industries, rather than crafts or professions (apart from the separate professional organizations, for example, teachers). All have a dual structure, part horizontal (geographical) and part vertical (industrial). Each contains about 30 federations and 90 UDs (unions départementales).

The machinery in every case provides for:

1 A confederal committee, representing all local unions and federations and meeting about twice a year.
2 An executive commission (known in the CFDT as 'national bureau'), consisting of about 30 representatives and meeting bi-monthly.
3 A confederal bureau of full-time officers (known in the CFDT as 'executive'), which is the organization's standing executive committee. It is usually made up of about 15 elected members and meets once a week.

All three confederations hold a congress, at two or three-yearly intervals, which elects the executive commission.

There has been evidence of a growing tendency towards greater centralization and the vesting of greater authority in the leadership. This is due to the increasing involvement of the unions in national economic and social affairs. The confederations are in fact more influential nationally than in individual establishments.

Another recent tendency has been towards increased inter-union cooperation. Until the late 1960s, the different confederations were bitterly opposed to each other and the CGT refused to have anything to do with what it regarded as its upstart rivals (apart from periods when the common front was the tactic). Since 1970, however, efforts have been made by CGT and CFDT to bring about a greater degree of working unity.

Reasonably amicable working arrangements are usually made at plant level, where questions of politics, religion and ideology are less important than the need to face the employer with a common front. This does not mean that there has been any lessening of inter-union competition for membership and prestige, but it does hamper any attempt by management to play off one union against another.

Nationally, a force making for a greater measure of common action has been the fact that the employers' organizations are affiliated to the Conseil national du patronat français. Having started mainly as a coodinating body for the various employer federations, the CNPF has been playing an increasingly active role in negotiations and in tripartite discussions with the government. As in Britain the several employers' federations negotiate on wages and hours with the counterpart trade unions. There are no political or ideological groupings within the CNPF. In recent years the CNPF leadership has aimed to play a progressive role on such matters as conditions and training.

Close relations have been established between the CGT and the CFDT on a pragmatic basis. A common programme was agreed between the two organizations in 1970, providing for joint action to secure higher minimum wages and cost of living escalation, earlier retirement and higher pensions, effective observance of the 40 hour week, new regional policies and investment in less developed areas.

The concordat was renewed in the autumn of 1972 and since then joint statements are issued periodically reaffirming the determination of the two organizations to carry on the campaign to raise minimum wages and help the lower-paid workers and pensioners as well as extending trade union rights. The two bodies are committed to coordinate their activities at every level.

The CGT also occasionally engages in common action with the CGC on questions of salaries. Both bodies are committed to maintaining differentials.

There is, however, no question of long-term unification. The CGT is still viewed with suspicion by non-Communist organizations and the CGT-FO has refused to entertain any idea of cooperation. CGT-FO also regards the CFDT as opportunist.

None of the trade union confederations is wealthy and union contributions are extremely low. The CGT, CGT-FO and the CFDT however all run well-produced weekly journals and issue regular propaganda material. The CGT popular monthly magazine for women *Antoinette* has a wide circulation.

For day-to-day activity, the confederations rely on the délégués syndicaux. These délégués syndicaux exist by virtue of a law of December 1968 and are nominated by the unions. Their number depends on the size of the establishment and they must be given certain facilities. In addition there are workers' delegates, or délégués du personnel, who are elected in all factories employing more than 10 people to represent the workers. They were introduced under a law of 1945.

Elections for workers' delegates are held annually. In the first ballot only candidates nominated by representative unions may be elected, but if no union lists are put forward or less than half the number of workers vote, a second ballot must be called in which non-unionists may stand. The number of delegates varies according to the size of the firm. Among their duties they present grievances to the employers and inform the Labour Inspectorate of any non-observance of regulations by the employer, and give their views on the internal working of the factory, safety, hygiene, holidays and ways of increasing production. They cooperate with the works council, of which they are usually themselves active members.

Both types of delegates are protected against wrongful dismissal. The employer is obliged to keep a notice board for union communications, put a room at their disposal, allow a certain period of time off (10-15 hours a month) and receive individual or collective deputations. The employer should record the delegate's representations and state within 6 days what action has been taken.

Collective Bargaining and Industrial Relations

There is not the same tradition of collective bargaining in France as in most EEC countries. The first comprehensive agreement was drawn up under the Popular Front government, the so-called 'Matignon' agreement of 1936. This encouraged the negotiation of industry-wide collective agreements, as well as providing for immediate increases in wages and salaries and extending the recognition of trade union rights. The present legal framework of collective bargaining was established in 1950, under an Act in which agreements can be concluded for an industry or an occupation. It introduced a minimum wage and established the principle of equal pay. Since 1952, the minimum wage (now called the salaire minimum interprofessionel de croissance, SMIC) has been linked to movements in the retail price index. It is also reviewed annually in the light of growth factors, for example, general movements in wages.

The 1950 Act encouraged the development of collective bargaining and by 1960, there were 189 national agreements in force. In the early part of the 1960s there was a slackening of interest and it was not until after the unrest of May 1968 that the government initiated a new drive. This produced what became known as the 'Grenelle' declaration, drawn up at a meeting between employers and union leaders under the auspices of the prime minister. After this, there was a rapid extension of collective bargaining, to cover such questions as hours, salaried status and profit-sharing.

In the 18 months following the declaration, 71 agreements on hours were reached for industries, where before May 1968 there had only been three such agreements.

Collective bargaining was applied with a new stimulus to employees in the public sector, for example the civil service and nationalized industries. Two important national agreements followed — one on job security and re-dundancy, and the other on training and further training.

The 1950 Act was brought up to date and strengthened by a new Act in July 1971. This Act contains 12 articles, with three main objectives:

1   To extend the practice of plant bargaining.
2   To widen the field covered by collective bargaining.
3   To strengthen the contractual basis of negotiation.

National agreements usually lay down minimum scales and run for a year, with the possibility of extension. In some industries, the national agreement is supplemented by regional or local agreements, for example textiles. In engineering there are no nationally negotiated rates, only regional and local agreements.

Contracts must stipulate the rates for various categories and the conditions of employment and dismissal, together with the period of notice. They may include arrangements for overtime, rest-day and shift work, rewards for productivity, long-service bonuses, indemnities for work changes, travel, etc. and arrangements for retirement.

Employers may negotiate individually or collectively with trade unions and these agreements are binding only on the signatories. If agreements are reached between the most representative employers' and workers' organizations they may, by decree of the Minister of Labour, be extended to cover a whole industry or occupation.

Plant bargaining is becoming an increasingly important feature.

The first serious plant agreement was drawn up at the Renault (nationalized) car factory in 1955. At first the unions opposed the system arguing, that where trade unions were weak, employers would be able to exploit the workers. But the benefits were held to outweigh the possible disadvantages and the system is popular with the workers who see in it a means of raising earnings and fringe benefits.

Collective agreements usually contain some provision for conciliation, but the state machinery for conciliation and arbitration is seldom used.

Disputes

The French have a reputation for being strike-prone, though as Figure 7:3 shows, the number of working days lost through disputes in France during the past decade is by no means the highest in the EEC countries. The right to strike is written into the Constitution. There are, however, some restrictions. Policemen, security police, prison officers and air traffic controllers are forbidden to strike. Despite these restrictions, which are not always faithfully observed, the French worker regards the strike weapon as his inalienable right. He may not by law be victimized for having taken part in a strike.

Industrial action to secure higher wages is concentrated in the actual bargaining period, in order to exert the maximum pressure on the employer and to influence the course of national bargaining by action at plant level. A characteristic of French strikes is their shortness and sporadic nature compared with those in most countries. In the last decade their average duration has been less than six days, but each strike usually involves about 1000 workers. Many of the CGT sponsored strikes are lightning one-day demonstrations, often for political reasons.

Figure 7:3 shows the strike record between 1962 and 1971.

In 1971 the biggest losses occurred in transport (1¼ million) and machinery and vehicles (nearly 500 000). These two sectors accounted for over 1½ million working days. Building and general engineering were also seriously affected by stoppages. One of the most strike-hit plants is the nationalized Renault car undertaking, which is a CGT bastion and is used to set the pace.

Wages are the most frequent cause of strikes, but there are frequent brief political and protest stoppages.

The method of sit-in which was a characteristic of the Popular Front period is still used, though to a lesser extent. Sometimes this action is accompanied by locking up the management and in 1972 about 40 such 'lock-ups' were reported. A new development, parallel to the occupation of Upper Clyde Shipyard and other British factories threatened with redundancies, was the move in the summer of 1973 by workers at the Lip watch factory in Besançon to carry on production and sales on their own, when they learned of a management plan to declare large-scale redundancies.

The Balance Sheet

It would be wrong to imagine that because the degree of trade unionization is low in France, and because of internal divisions, the unions are not powerful enough to have succeeded in achieving higher living standards. Because they operate militantly in strategically important sectors of the

economy, such as engineering, transport, and electricity, they are in a strong
position to enforce their demands and to set the pace for other industries.
They have also concluded agreements with the CNPF on matters left by
British unions to the government, such as unemployment insurance and
vocational training. The very existence of inter-union rivalry leads to an
all-round raising of sights and employers, individually or collectively, have
been unable to resist the pressure.

During the 1960s, industrial earnings rose more steeply than in any other
EEC country. Taking 1964 as 100, the earnings index reached 181 in 1971
and during 1972 France experienced the steepest rise in hourly rates (12 per

Figure 7:3   Industrial disputes in France

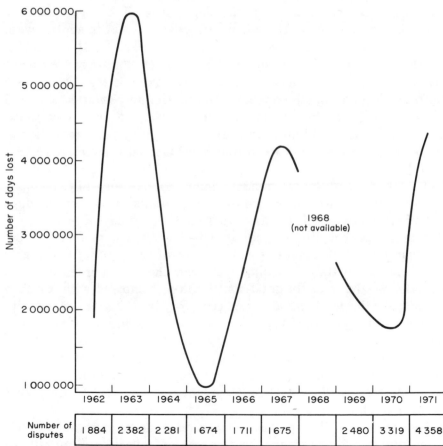

Number of disputes	1962	1963	1964	1965	1966	1967	1968	1969	1970	1971
	1 884	2 382	2 281	1 674	1 711	1 675		2 480	3 319	4 358

Source: *ILO Yearbook of Labour Statistics*, 1972

cent) since 1957. This was due to the workers' pressure to counter the rapid price inflation, the highest of any Common Market country. During the 1960s, the price index rose from 100 (1963) to 133 and the rise continued more steeply in the early 1970s.

In 1970 the general index of consumer prices went up, by 5.2 per cent over the previous year; in 1971 by 5.5 per cent and in 1972 by 6.1 per cent. The main cause of the increase was the rise in food prices, particularly that of meat.

To combat price inflation the government in December 1972 introduced its 'plan anti-hausse' which included cuts in VAT rates, the issue of a national loan worth Fr 5000 million, a tightening of credit and the encouragement of savings. The government also recommended employers and labour to limit the rate of pay increases to 6 per cent during 1973. This was on the assumption that if price rises could be held to 4 per cent there would be a 2 per cent gain in purchasing power. The suggestion was over-optmistic from the start. There is no effective attempt to control wage rises.

Although France was the first country to introduce the forty-hour week in principle the number of hours actually worked exceeds this. Overtime is payable from 40 hours in all industries. The maximum permitted standard working week is 54 hours, including overtime for a 5 or 6 day week. Collective agreements in various industries aim at a progressive reduction in hours worked. Average hours worked (industrial manual workers) were 43.8 in January 1973.

French workers enjoy longer holidays than those of any EEC country, except Italy. Annual leave, laid down by law, amounts to 24 working days plus 8-10 public holidays. The total ranges from 32 to 34 days a year.

As far as fringe benefits are concerned, the French system is more generous than most EEC countries and the cost of social benefits is higher than anywhere except Italy. The employer bears the main burden of costs, paying nearly two-thirds of the total contribution, compared with less than 25 per cent for the worker and 7 per cent for the state. Social security benefits cover old age, invalidity, death, sickness, maternity, occupational injury and family allowances. Benefits are wage-related. There is no national health service, but insured persons can recoup 75-80 per cent of the cost of medical treatment, pharmaceutical costs and hospitalization (100 per cent in the case of protracted illness). Unemployment insurance is run by a joint CNPF-trade union body.

As elsewhere in the EEC, provision has been made to 'cushion' workers against the effects of redundancy. In the case of collective dismissals for 'technical or economic reasons' (for example lack of raw materials, market changes, reorganization or the introduction of new techniques) arrangements for advance notification and compensation are made. An employer must inform the appropriate labour authorities and, if possible, give priority to the dismissed workers if there is a revival of employment. Members of the works council like the workers' 'delegates' cannot be dismissed without the approval of the Labour Inspectorate.

An important development, which France has pioneered, is the transference of weekly or fortnightly paid manual workers to salaried status, with payment of wages on a monthly basis. This process known as 'mensualisation' gathered impetus after the May 1968 troubles. It was blessed by President Pompidou, then Prime Minister, who expressed the hope that it would provide greater security and a new dignity for working people. By the end of 1969, about 1 million manual workers were on a salaried basis and it is estimated that by the end of 1974 more than 4 million will be covered. Agreements have been reached in the major industries, including iron and steel, chemicals, building, textiles and many consumer goods industries.

The change is more a matter of improved status than of concrete benefits, though in such subjects as sick leave, rest periods, entitlement to pensions, there are positive advantages. It has meant the end of clocking-in for factory workers at Renault.

Mensualisation will add to employers' costs, though the amount cannot be precisely estimated; one important effect should be to arrest the tendency for workers to take up white-collar salaried rather than skilled manual jobs. In changing personal habits, for example, the use of cheque books, the process could have important social effects.

Cooperation

The majority of French trade unionists have a long tradition of militancy and opposition to the capitalist system. The revolutionary doctrines of the CGT and the CFDT make it impossible for employers to have the same sort of relations with the unions as exist in Germany. The events of may 1968, still fresh in people's minds, have left a legacy of mutual mistrust and apprehension. Among employers, there are many smaller 'patrons' who regard trade unionists as irresponsible and refuse to concede their rights, even though this is against the law. But on the whole, largely as a result of the extension of collective bargaining procedures, a better employer-worker relationship has been brought about. This is reflected on the employers' side by an increased interest in management and business courses, where industrial relations feature on the agenda and the accent is on human understanding. In the recent past the initiative for better relations has come from the CNPF. Among some workers' leaders there is a growing realization that they are more likely to win concessions round the board-room table than at the factory gates, but the strike weapon is kept ready in order to exert any necessary extra pressure. However the continuance of material prosperity is making it more difficult for the militant unions to mobilize their members for industrial action.

A parallel development was the setting up in 1969 of joint employer/ union commissions for each industry, to study employment and training matters. This was followed in 1970 by an important bilateral agreement on training and further training, which clearly recognized that the content conditions and terms of training were a matter of joint responsibility. This radical approach to the problem was given statutory backing by the Act of July 1971.

Since the end of the Second World War, France has had a system of compulsory works councils (comités d'entreprise) set up by the Act of 1945. These councils are obligatory in any establishment with more than 50 employees. Elections are held every two years and the number of representatives varies according to the total workforce of the factory. Only representative trade unions may nominate candidates, but if the unions fail to present lists or less than half the workers vote, a second ballot is held, in which non-unionists may stand. The councils meet at least once a month in the employer's time and on his premises. They are consultative and discuss such issues as working conditions, training and deployment of labour, production and productivity and dismissals. The councils run the firm's social activities, for example, canteens, holiday facilities and welfare. The employer is obliged to provide information about the firm's programme and employment prospects as well as its financial situation. Members of the council cannot be dismissed without the consent of the Labour Inspectorate. In addition there are hygiene and safety committees – and the workers' representatives are usually nominated by the works council.

The effectiveness of the councils varies enormously. In some firms, where workers are unorganized, they barely function. In the past the left-wing unions tended to denigrate them as an ineffective form of control, but recently both the CGT and the CFDT have begun to realize their potential and seek to make them more than talking-shops. Managements have not been over-enthusiastic about the councils, regarding them as time-consuming and unnecessary additions to their already heavy burdens.

The legislation on 'participation in profits' has given a new stimulus to the committees, as these need to approve the investment of the funds involved. The committees are entitled to nominate two or four representatives, according to the size of the company, as observers to the board of their firm. They do not vote and their presence is regarded as something of a formality. The Prime Minister has, however, now promised that these representatives will be given voting powers.

In 1967 a compulsory profit-sharing scheme was introduced in all firms with more than 100 workers. The scheme is complicated and has not been particularly popular either with the employers or the workers. It provides that after meeting salaries and overheads and a maximum of 5 per cent set aside for return on capital, the balance is shared out among the employees. The funds are invested and workers must wait for 5 years initially before taking their share.

It is designed to increase the worker's sense of identity with his company.

In France, successive governments as has been shown in this chapter, have played a major part in encouraging collective bargaining and workers' participation in industry, and have sought to improve the climate of industrial relations and promote 'social peace'. Because of internal union divisions and the ideological antipathy between the employers and the main confederations government intervention has been more active than might have been the case had the unions been centralized and 'moderated', as in Germany.

There is provision for consultation on various aspects of labour and social legislation on the tripartite statutory Economic and Social Council.

The French employment and industrial relations system incorporates a degree of legislation which would not be acceptable in the United Kingdom. It is universally accepted that such matters as the protection of workers' health and safety are appropriate subjects for legislation. But in France there are laws covering the contract of employment, works councils, profit-sharing, salaried status and many other matters which would be dealt with on a voluntary basis in Britain, or which would be regarded as a matter of civil law or administrative action.

There is legislation on a national minimum wage, social security, holidays with pay, hours and equal pay. The whole system is codified in a detailed comprehensive Code du travail, the enforcement of which comes under the Ministry of Labour, Employment and Population, through its regional and departmental inspectorate.

The Act of July 1971 for professional retraining provides a comprehensive and radical basis for retraining at all levels. As part of these facilities the

National Association for the Training of Adults runs training courses on behalf of the Ministry of Labour.

In all these ways the French government exercises what it would regard as a guiding light and benevolent oversight of developments in industrial and social relations, encouraging and stimulating the 'social partners' to accept their responsibilities. Most Frenchmen, whether employers or workers, do not like government intervention and seek to evade it if they can. But at the current stage of development and until collective bargaining has really taken root, it is generally recognized that some such intervention is necessary for the nation's economic health.

8

Federal Republic of Germany

Economic Background

With about 61 million inhabitants, including West Berlin, the Federal Republic of Germany has the largest population of the nine EEC countries. In size — its land area covers 250 000 square kilometres — it is surpassed by France and Italy. Density, at 248 inhabitants to the square kilometre, is the third highest in the EEC.

Three cities have populations of over 1 million — West Berlin (2 163 000), Hamburg (1 833 000) and Munich (1 244 000). Bonn, the capital, has 138 000 inhabitants. Other important cities are Cologne (854 000), Essen (705 000), Düsseldorf (689 000), Frankfurt (622 000), Dortmund (648 000), Stuttgart (614 000) and Bremen (604 000).

Employment

The working population totals about 23 million, of whom 8.6 million are engaged in industry. Women represent about 50 per cent of the working population. The number of workers employed in agriculture have been declining and represent about 8 per cent of the workforce.

Heavy industries have traditionally been part of the nation's economic structure, largely based in the Ruhr, Rhineland and Hamburg areas. Traditional industries like coal have declined but this has been offset by the growth of modern technological and consumer-oriented industries. Hanover in the northeast and Stuttgart in the southwest have become increasingly important industrial centres. Flourishing sectors of the West German economy include vehicles, chemicals and plastics, electro-technical industries, oil and petro-chemicals, textiles, precision and optical instruments.

In recent years the unemployment rate has remained below 1 per cent of the working population.

Figure 8:1   Analysis of employment by principal sectors

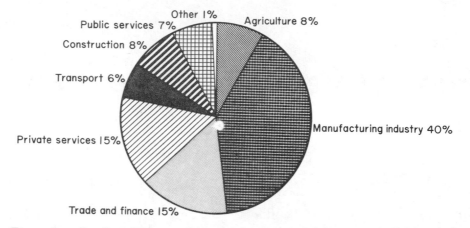

There has in fact been a chronic shortage of labour and Germany has imported large numbers of immigrant workers, mainly from Italy and the non EEC Mediterranean countries. The present number of foreign workers is over 2 million, representing about 10 per cent of the total labour force.

The Economy

West Germany has been the most prosperous and economically stable member of the EEC since its foundation. Between 1950 and 1970 the Federal Republic achieved an economic growth rate of 6.5 per cent per annum and became the world's second largest trading nation (after the USA).

There was a mild recession in 1970 and in 1971 and 1972 the annual growth rate was less than 3 per cent. However, the trend in 1973 was expected to produce a rate of about 5 per cent and some experts predict as high a rate as 7 per cent.

The latest GNP figure (1970) is £97 500 million.

West Germany has enjoyed a consistently healthy balance of payments. Though there is a net outflow of invisibles in the form of tourists' expenditure abroad and remittances by immigrant workers, the current account continues to be in surplus. Its main markets are in the EEC countries, headed by France and the Netherlands and its chief exports are machinery, vehicles, chemicals, electrical equipment, textiles, precision

Population density in principal regions

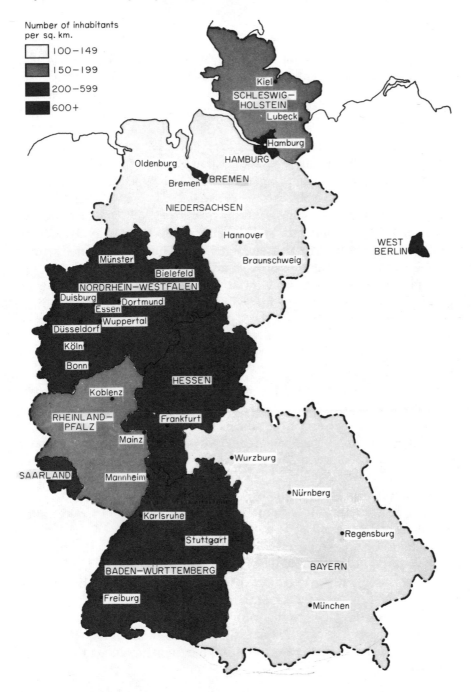

Number of inhabitants
per sq. km.

- ☐ 100–149
- ▨ 150–199
- ▉ 200–599
- ⬛ 600+

SCHLESWIG–
HOLSTEIN

Kiel

Lübeck

Hamburg

HAMBURG

Oldenburg

Bremen

BREMEN

NIEDERSACHSEN

Hannover

Braunschweig

WEST
BERLIN

Münster

Bielefeld

NORDRHEIN–WESTFALEN

Duisburg

Essen

Dortmund

Wuppertal

Düsseldorf

Köln

Bonn

HESSEN

Koblenz

RHEINLAND–
PFALZ

Frankfurt

Mainz

Wurzburg

SAARLAND

Mannheim

Nürnberg

Karlsruhe

Regensburg

Stuttgart

BADEN–WÜRTTEMBERG

BAYERN

Freiburg

München

instruments and optical and photo-mechanical products.

Government

West Germany is a federal republic, headed by an elected president. There are 10 Länder (state parliaments), which are represented in the upper house, or Bundesrat. The lower chamber, the Bundestag, has 518 members elected by universal suffrage on proportional representation.

The Bundestag has powers over defence, foreign affairs, transport and federal finance, but each Land is otherwise autonomous. There are two major parties in the Bundestag — the Christian Democrats (CDU) and the Social Democrats (SDP). A smaller third, Liberal type party, the Free Democrats, holds between 30-50 seats.

The Christian Democrats held power from 1949 to 1969, when a coalition of the SDP and Free Democrats was formed with Herr Willy Brandt as Chancellor. This coalition had a very small majority, but was returned with a majority of 46 seats in the election of November 1972.

The federal President holds no power, and the Chancellor cannot be dismissed by the Bundestag except by a vote which simultaneously appoints his successor.

Membership

Trade unions were banned under the Nazi regime, which confiscated their funds and interned, deported or executed many of their leaders. One of the first tasks facing the new German nation after the Second World War was to reconstruct the trade union movement on a strong, unified and democratic basis. Before 1933, there were some 200 different organizations and there were divisions on craft, ideological and religious lines. Because there had been no free unions for 15 years and few of the labour leaders had survived, reconstruction had to be done from scratch. The British TUC gave considerable help in the process.

The regrouping of unions into 16 main organizations began immediately after the Second World War and culminated in the foundation of the German TUC, the Deutsche Gewerkschaftsbund (DGB) at Munich in 1949. Its first president was the veteran Hans Böckler.

Figure 8:2 shows the DGB membership, by industrial grouping, in 1962 and 1972. The dominant organization is the Metalworkers Union (IG Metall Union) which has nearly one third of the total membership and is the biggest in the western world.

Figure 8:2   German Trade Union Federation (DGB) membership at 31 December 1972

Union	Manual workers	Non-manual workers	Total male	Total female	Grand total male & female	Percentage of total union members	Total membership in 1962
Building, quarrying and public works contracting	488 362	32 517	515 812	5 067	520 879	7.5	444 000
Mine and power workers	335 554	44 990	375 838	4 993	380 831	5.4	504 000
Chemical, paper and pottery workers	533 266	93 505	518 431	108 340	626 771	9.0	527 000
Printing and paper processing	139 438	13 969	124 247	29 160	153 407	2.2	146 000
Railwaymen	253 913	10 463	420 017	14 872	434 889	6.2	434 000
Education and scientific workers	—	19 182	76 095	49 650	125 745	1.8	88 000
Horticultural, agricultural and forestry	36 795	2 089	39 894	1 950	41 844	0.6	78 000
Salaried employees, trade, commerce and banking	32 543	158 528	98 561	92 510	191 071	2.7	127 000
Woodworkers	123 706	7 099	119 451	11 354	130 805	1.9	148 000
Artists and entertainments	—	35 344	26 150	9 194	35 344	0.5	32 000
Leatherworkers	56 791	2 364	36 215	22 940	59 155	0.8	86 000
Metalworkers	2 070 423	284 552	2 087 236	267 739	2 354 975	33.7	1 528 000
Food, drink, tobacco and catering	216 816	32 852	176 376	73 292	249 668	3.6	282 000
Public services, transport and communications	536 644	350 813	813 562	184 209	997 771	14.3	984 000
Postal workers	110 166	33 404	306 191	84 597	390 788	5.6	307 000
Textile and clothing	272 473	19 132	136 206	155 399	291 605	4.2	341 000
DGB – Grand total:	5 188 890 74.3%	1 140 803 16.3%	5 870 282 84 %	1 115 266 16 %	6 985 548 100%	100%	6 056 000

In addition, there are a few independent non-DGB organizations. A separate union has been formed for white-collar workers (DAG) with about 500 000 members – though many salaried employees belong to DGB unions. The civil servants' union (DBB) has over 700 000 members. The police are organized in a union with about 100 000 members. The Christian tradition is represented by the continued existence of the Christliche Gewerkschaftsbund Deutschland (CGB) with 200 000 members.

Total membership of DGB and non-DGB unions is about 8 million, or one-third of the labour force of about 23 million. The DGB figure includes about 1 million women, and 600 000 young workers between 14 and 21.

Union membership has remained remarkably constant. When the DGB was first set up it had 4.9 million members, and the figure rose to 6 million in 1952. Since that date it has fluctuated between the 6 and 7 million mark. The failure to increase membership is a major problem for the DGB. Workers in engineering, transport and mining are strongly organized, but membership is low in agriculture and trade. Many German workers feel that they can get the benefits of trade union action without having to join, while many on the left-wing regard the machinery as bureaucratic and conservative.

Structure

German workers are organized in industrial unions and all the employees in one plant belong to the same union. The Metalworkers Union includes not only engineering workers, but workers in iron and steel, shipbuilding, electro-technical, computers and atomic energy; it also includes masons, joiners and commercial and technical staffs.

The unified structure means the elimination of demarcation problems and facilitates negotiations. An exception is where a proportion of staff belong to the DAG, which involves two separate sets of negotiation.

The individual unions are financially autonomous and conduct their own wage negotiations. Structurally, they follow the same pattern as the DGB, with local, regional and national offices. Their structure is centralized and hierarchical and most of them are wealthy. Individual unions contribute 12 per cent of their members' dues to the central organization. The worker's union contribution is generally set at the equivalent of 1 hour's work a week, and this is often deducted at source from the pay packet.

Most of the big unions run regular newspapers and spend a great deal of money on training. IG Metall, for example, has its own education centre at Bochum.

The DGB

The DGB exercises a greater national authority and influence over its affiliates than in any EEC country. When it was founded in 1949 it adopted a four-point charter, stressing demands for full employment and maximum efficiency in the use of national resources, codetermination with management, nationalization of key industries, a fair share in the national economic product and help for the elderly, the sick and the disabled. These basic principles were reaffirmed and extended at a special conference in Düsseldorf in 1963, when even more stress was laid on economic expansion and the worker's right to share in increased prosperity.

The DGB and its affiliated unions are independent of any political party, though they are primarily Social-democrat in outlook. Despite the absence of formal links, the unions are politically very powerful. In the present federal parliament, over half the deputies belong to trade unions and in the cabinet of Herr Willy Brandt, ten ministers are union members.

Individual unions pursue their own economic policies but the DGB acts as a powerful coordinating and educative body. It helps the smaller unions, which do not have the resources of the giants, such as the Metalworkers Union, with advice and assistance on legal problems, social security and education. At national level, the DGB is the spokesman for the entire trade union movement.

Its supreme governing body is the federal congress, whose delegates are elected by member unions in proportion to their strength. The congress meets every three years and in between, DGB affairs are run by an executive national committee consisting of the president, two vice-presidents and six other members. The DGB's huge glass and concrete headquarters at Düsseldorf (erected in 1967 at the cost of about 20 million DM) is divided into eight departments (economic, finance, vocational training and women, education and collective bargaining, social policy, organization and youth, publicity and salaried employees, and civil servants). Each comes under the direction of one of the executive members. The national committee meets several times a month.

In the country, the DGB has its regional offices (Baden-Württemberg, Bavaria, Berlin, Hesse, Lower Saxony, Northmark, North Rhine-Westphalia, the Rhineland Palatinate and the Saar). Regional conferences are held regularly and delegates are elected by individual trade unions which are also represented on the regional presidium. The DGB has offices and branches in about 300 towns and centres.

German unions are big business and they have entered into many fields associated with private enterprise. For example, in 1958, they formed a Bank für Gemeinwirtschaft, which is the fourth largest private bank in the country. The unions' Neue Heimat Building Society has built some 400 000 houses to accommodate over a million people and is now engaged in building hospitals, town halls, nursery schools, swimming pools and shopping centres. The DGB and its unions operate an insurance company, Volksfürsorge, covering every aspect of personal and business insurance. Other DGB interests include a holiday and travel agency, a book and record publishing business, an automobile club and a chain of over 5000 food and furniture shops, including supermarkets, department stores, and factories producing household goods.

The DGB is also involved in publishing. It produces a weekly newspaper and special periodicals for young workers, white-collar workers, civil servants and economists and other groups. It has a large and efficient research section and runs many training schools for union officials and executives. About 25 000 trade unionists attend courses every year. The unions also support high-level academies at Frankfurt, Dortmund and Hamburg Universities.

In these and other ways, the German trade unions are demonstrating that they can run large-scale economic and social enterprises in the interests of their members and in competition with private institutions. It is part of their philosophy of cooperation within the framework of the capitalist system, rather than seeking to overthrow it, which is still the declared objective of many European labour movements. The unions' aim is to increase productivity, encourage technological progress and ensure that the workers' share in national prosperity is increased.

The DGB maintains good relations with the employers' organization responsible for labour and social matters, the Bundesvereinigung des Deutschen Arbeitgeberverbände, (BDA). This central body was set up shortly after the foundation of the DGB, partly to counter the growing strength of the union organizations. The employers' confederation comprises about 800 different associations in every branch of the economy. It does not negotiate directly with the unions, but lays down broad guidelines and suggests model agreements to its constituents. It speaks for all employers *vis-à-vis* the government on labour and social matters.

Collective Bargaining and Industrial Relations

The German worker is guaranteed freedom of association under the Constitution. This provides that there shall exist for 'every man and for all callings . . . the right to form associations for the preservation and advancement of conditions of employment and economic activity'. The Law also recognizes an individual's right not to belong to a union and the closed shop is illegal.

Wages are normally determined by collective bargaining, which may be on an industry or nation-wide basis. The right of collective bargaining is guaranteed under the Constitution and the Collective Agreements Act of 1949. A collective agreement does not need government approval, although agreements have to be reported to the Federal Minister of Labour. Collective agreements, however, are legally binding under the 1949 Act, as amended in 1969. The government has no right to intervene in collective bargaining.

Neither the DGB nor the BDA intervene in the course of negotiations, but both bodies have recently increasingly issued guidelines to their affiliated organizations, in an effort to coordinate wage movements.

Agreements usually lay down minimum wages and working conditions and most agreements usually include provisions for conciliation, based on a model procedure agreement reached between the DGB and the BDA in 1954. There is no provision for compulsory conciliation or arbitration which is purely voluntary. Labour courts at local, provincial or federal level are responsible for the enforcement of collective agreements.

These labour courts form an integral part of the German industrial relations structure. They were originally established in the 1920s and their operation is governed by the Labour Court Act of 1953, which established a three-tier system of local and regional courts and a Federal Labour Court. They are composed of a qualified judge as chairman, plus two to four assessors from both sides of industry. The judges have to be well-versed in industrial relations procedures and labour law. The courts adjudicate on disputes arising from contracts of employment, collective agreements and the Works Constitution Act. Nine in ten legal actions have to do with claims by individual workers against employers, mostly over pay, dismissals and redundancy. A worker may represent himself or be represented by his union. The atmosphere in the courts is usually informal and most cases are settled amicably, with the judge and his assessors acting as conciliators.

In North Rhine-Westphalia in 1972, over 31 000 cases were settled by 32 local courts and only 4000 involved formal judgments.

Both sides of industry broadly accept the system as a useful method of ensuring the observance of collective contracts and it is generally agreed that the labour courts contribute to the maintenance of industrial peace.

During the currency of a collective agreement, which is usually for 1-2 years, both sides are legally bound to maintain 'social peace'. Neither strikes nor lock-outs are allowed and penalties for any breach can be quite high. The result is that such action as the unions may take occurs in the period leading up to the conclusion of a bargain, with the object of bringing maximum pressure on the employers. The unions, as 'social partners', are well aware of their obligations and the need to observe binding collective agreements. Unconstitutional strikes are unlawful.

Disputes

Largely because of the discipline imposed by the unions and their sense of social responsibility, the German workers have been the least strike-prone of any within the EEC. The right to strike is implicitly but not explicitly recognized under the Constitution, but the strike weapon is regarded as a last resort, not to be used except in extreme circumstances. According to DGB guidelines, a strike may not be called unless 75 per cent of union members have voted for industrial action in a secret ballot. Then a strike must be formally authorized by the union, which has to weigh up the various economic and social factors involved. Once a strike has been called, trade unions pay fairly high strike benefit. Members of the Metalworkers Union, for example, can receive £16-20 a week strike pay, according to the length of their membership. If necessary the DGB will subvent a union through its special solidarity fund. Sympathetic strikes and political strikes are ruled out, and proved intimidation by pickets would render an otherwise lawful strike illegal.

Most strikes in Germany since the end of the Second World War have been of short duration. An exception was the metalworkers strike in Baden-Württemberg in 1972 which contributed to a total loss of 3 million working days. Serious, and at times violent, wildcat strikes took place at the Ford plant at Köln and in other engineering plants in the Ruhr. These were attributed by official leaders as having been fomented by 'outside agitators'.

Figure 8:3 shows the number of working days lost, by main industrial groups during the past decade.

The Balance Sheet

The policy of cooperation in order to produce economic expansion has paid handsome dividends. German workers enjoy a high material standard of living as measured, for example, by the numbers of cars, TV sets and food consumption of the population — although there are still regional disparities.

Average weekly earnings are between £45-50. Miners earn £43, electricians £44, bus drivers £47 and car workers £49. Dock workers and teachers are among the highest paid, with £56 and £67 a week average respectively.

At the same time, wage rises have been reduced in value by the continued increase in prices.

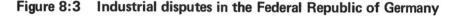

Figure 8:3   Industrial disputes in the Federal Republic of Germany

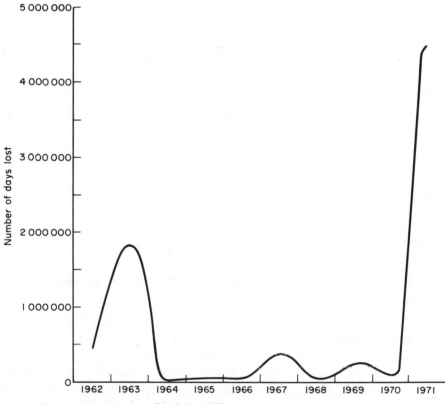

Source: *ILO Yearbook of Labour Statistics,* 1972

German unions are as much concerned about fringe benefits and social welfare as about the size of the pay packet. The national social insurance system, which dates from Bismarck's day, offers comprehensive coverage against illness, accidents, retirement and unemployment. It covers about 95 per cent of the entire population and is supplemented by a scheme of social assistance. Apart from industrial injuries, the cost is divided between employers and employees, contributions and benefits are related to incomes.

All the schemes are operated by independent self-governing bodies, usually composed of equal numbers of workers' and employers' representatives. The government's role is limited to legal supervision. This system gives the German unions a vital stake in the administration and extension of social security, and means that public funds amounting to about one quarter of the total GNP are largely managed by the two sides of industry.

The total expenditure on the social budget rose from £19 million in 1971 to £27 million in 1972 and is planned to increase to £38 million by 1976. Over a third of the increase is accounted for by old age pensions, since the elderly constitute a large part of the population.

As far as hours and holidays are concerned, German workers are not as liberally treated as their opposite numbers in France and Italy. In April 1972, the average working week, for men and women, was 43.1 hours, compared with 44.2 in 1970 and 42.2 in April 1967. Holidays with pay are between 3 and 4 weeks a year, and there are 10-13 public holidays, according to the regions. In some industries there are schemes for long-service workers to take additional days' leave.

Cooperation

One of the main pillars of the West German unions' philosophy is their belief in workers' codetermination or 'Mitbestimmung'. Their object is officially stated to be to 'ensure that every citizen will be enabled to participate on a basis of full equality in every economic, cultural and political decision affecting his country'.

There is a long tradition of consultation and cooperation. The first works councils were actually set up in the 1920s, though they ceased to function after 1933. As part of the postwar social reconstruction, the system was reintroduced with a series of legal enactments. The Codetermination Law of 1951 provides for equal representation of shareholders and workers on the supervisory board (Aufsichtsrat) of the coal and steel industries. In these industries, as elsewhere a two-tier system operates – a supervisory board and an executive or management board (Vorstand). The Aufsichtsrat decides basic overall policy but its members do not intervene in day-to-day management. This is the responsibility of the Vorstand, which includes a labour director, appointed with the approval of the worker members of the Aufsichtsrat.

In most supervisory boards in coal and steel, membership consists of 11, 15 or 21 people, and as well as the equal representation of the two sides of industry, there is a 'neutral' member coopted by the two sides.

In 1952, the Works Constitution Act provided for one-third representation of workers on the supervisory board of joint stock companies and all other limited companies with more than 500 workers. It does not provide for the appointment of a labour director, however, and unions have been pressing for parity, as in the coal and steel industries.

A similar system was extended to public services under the Personnel Representation Law of 1954.

The Works Constitution Act of 1952 was replaced in 1972 by a new Act, introduced by the Socialist-led coalition government. The 1952 Act had required every plant with more than 5 employees to have a workers' representative and those with more than 20 employees to establish a works council. The 1972 Act increased the influence of the councils.

Members are elected for three years. They do not have to be trade unionists, but in practice they usually are. It is estimated that about 180 000 workers are involved in works council activities. They are not joint bodies, but exclusively represent the workers.

Members enjoy special protection and privileges. They must be given time to attend meetings and, in large companies, they may be allowed to concentrate exclusively on council matters. The employer must provide an office, a meeting place and secretarial assistance and meet the costs involved. Each member is entitled during his first term of office to four weeks' paid leave to attend courses of further education and training – in a subsequent term the period is three weeks.

Works councils have certain clearly laid down duties. They have to be consulted on all social, personnel and industrial matters and on such questions as job evaluation, piece-rates and wages structures, working times, breaks and holiday arrangements. They are jointly responsible for training, safety and welfare, and play a part in the allocation of houses and flats provided by the employer. They also have disciplinary functions at shopfloor level.

An employer cannot hire, fire or promote a worker without the prior consent of the council, which must also approve matters involving manpower deployment, transfers and work regrouping, An employer is bound by law to give the council the reasons for dismissing a worker and the council has the right to object, for example, on grounds of 'social hardship'. Any disputes are referred to the appropriate labour court and no worker can be dismissed while his case is being considered. The employer must also give advance notice of any plan for redundancies, and may not reduce his labour force, alter the scale of operations or remove his plant without the council's consent.

In firms with more than 100 workers, the council appoints an economic committee of 4-8 members, which is entitled to receive full information on all matters involving finance, production and technical change.

Any difference within a 'codetermination area' can be referred by either party to independent arbitration. Where statutory rights are involved, the final decision rests with the labour courts.

In order to avoid a 'We' and 'They' atmosphere, the workers' representatives must report back to a works assembly every three months — held during working time.

The employers accepted the codetermination system when it was originally introduced, but strongly opposed the extensions proposed in the 1972 Act, particularly the idea of equal representation of workers and shareholders on private industries' supervisory boards. In a report criticizing the scheme, the BDA declared: 'By multiplying the number of bodies and procedures, it carries the risk of bureaucratizing, complicating and slowing down the process of managerial decision-making in a manner which may seriously affect the competitiveness of the German economy'. However, in the same report, the employers appealed to all managements to continue to cooperate with the works councils 'in a spirit of conciliation and responsibility'.

It is too early to assess the effect of the 1972 Act, but the Biedenkopf Commission which reported in 1970 found that codetermination had stood the test of practice and that the workers' representatives on the supervisory boards were in the main anxious to increase their company's profitability, realizing that job security depended on this.

The system has certainly increased the workers' sense of industrial participation and helped to maintain industrial peace. Many believe it to be a main factor in producing Germany's relative absence of strikes.

Another form of participation is represented by the various schemes to encourage savings and to enable workpeople to share in capital formation and the fruits of increased productivity. The system of tax rebates to encourage voluntary savings is encouraged by the unions. There is a scheme for an investment wage, amounting to a maximum of 312 DM tax free for workers under the so-called 'Law on the promotion of the accumulation of wealth by workpeople'. By the late 1960s there were 60 such collective agreements, affecting nearly 2 million workers, the majority being in the building industry. The unions' attitude to this scheme is that it should be regarded as a bonus payment and not as a form of compulsory saving. They prefer wider 'property-sharing' plans under which larger companies pay into a special fund a certain percentage of their annual profits, which would then be allocated among the workers after a given period.

Germany's workers are covered by laws and regulations affecting nearly every aspect of their industrial and social life. Their right to collective bargaining, to freedom of association and to works representation are all guaranteed by law, and there is also elaborate machinery for statutory protection in social security and factory health and welfare. Yet, the government itself has been extremely anxious not to intervene in the course of industrial relations or collective bargaining, but rather to encourage the two sides to come together in joint endeavours. The federal government sees its role as primarily to inform and advise the 'social partners' about the current economic situation and prospects. It publishes annual reports on the general economic situation and since 1970 has held a series of 'concerted action' policy talks with employers, trade unionists, as well as independent economists and the representatives of social insurance institutions. According to the federal Minister of Labour 'the purpose of this concerted action is not to negotiate specific prices and wages; it is to promote understanding and especially the realization that there is a limit between the reasonable interests of individual groups and economic necessities'.

In recent years, the government has been increasingly concerned about the growth of inflationary pressures and has advised negotiators to limit the rate of wage increases — without much effect. Whether, and to what extent, the government will be forced by economic circumstances to take a more direct hand in shaping wages and industrial relations policies will largely depend on the continued policy of cooperation between the two sides of industry in the public interest. There have been some signs of impatience and restlessness among some of the more militant and younger trade-unionists — the wildcat strikes in the metalworking industry in 1969 and 1973 were as much against union authority as against the employers.

9

Republic of Ireland

Economic Background

The land area of the Republic of Ireland is twice as large as that of the Netherlands, with 69 000 square kilometres. Its population, however, is very small and totalled just under 3 million at the latest census. Population density is low at 41 people per square kilometre.

Dublin, the capital, has a population of 568 000. Major towns are Cork (129 000), Limerick (57 000) and Waterford (32 000).

English and Gaelic are both official languages, but English is used for business purposes.

Employment

Industrialization has been slow in Ireland until recent years and in the early 1970s, about one third of the working population of about 1 million were employed in agriculture. The services sector is relatively small.

Two of the Republic's most important industries are directly related to agriculture — food, and drink. The metals and engineering section is second largest in terms of gross output. The manufacturing sector is primarily concerned with the processing of food and agricultural products, but the government has pursued an active policy of industrial development and diversification. Considerable financial and other concessions have been offered and have been successful in attracting overseas investment in a wide range of industries.

Tourism has been an important source of revenue but the troubles in the

North during the early 1970s affected the number of visitors.

Unemployment averaged about 6 per cent of the working population in 1971.

Figure 9:1 Analysis of employment by principal sectors

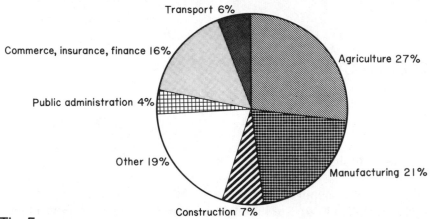

The Economy

The GNP was £1892 million in 1971. The economy grew rapidly during the 1960s at an average rate of 4.7 per cent per annum. Considerable fluctuations occurred during the end of the period and the rate slowed to 2.4 per cent in 1970, recovering to about 3 per cent in 1971 and 1972. With a high level of government spending under way, growth rates for 1973 and 1974 were expected to be in the order of 5 per cent.

Ireland's persistent balance of payments deficit is only partly alleviated by tourist earnings, emigrants' remittances and returns on investment abroad. The Republic is economically heavily dependent on Britain, which accounts for about 60 per cent of its exports and about 50 per cent of its imports. The Irish government hoped that a result of entry into the Common Market, this excessive dependency would be reduced and trading opportunities broadened.

Government

The Irish political system is based on two-chamber legislation – the Dail (with 144 members), and the Senate, (with 60). An elected President is head of state.

Population density in principal regions

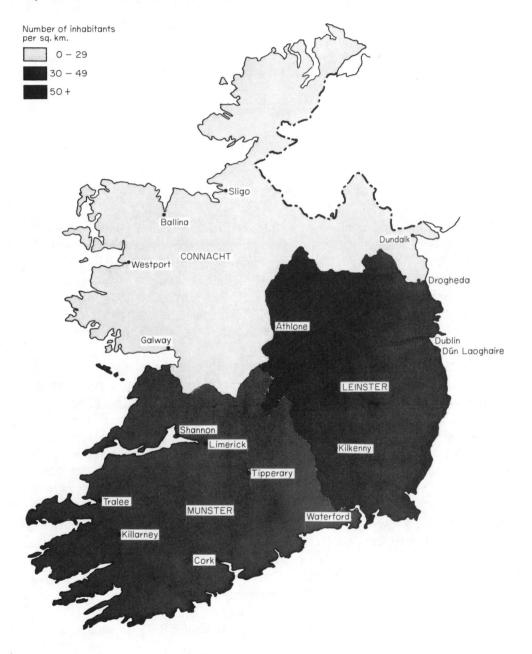

Number of inhabitants
per sq. km.

0 – 29

30 – 49

50 +

Sligo

Ballina

Dundalk

CONNACHT

Westport

Drogheda

Athlone

Galway

Dublin
Dún Laoghaire

LEINSTER

Shannon

Limerick

Kilkenny

Tipperary

Tralee

MUNSTER

Waterford

Killarney

Cork

The constitution provides for the use of referenda — one was used in 1972 to determine Common Market entry.

For 16 years, until February 1973, the Fianna Fáil party (broadly conservative) remained in power, in the last few years under the leadership of Mr John Lynch. The party was defeated in the 1973 election, when a coalition between Fine Gael and Labour achieved power. The present Prime Minister is Mr Liam Cosgrave. The Cosgrave government is basically Social-democrat and its policies include plans for increased welfare payments and social benefits. Mr Erskine Childers succeeded Mr de Valera as President in 1973.

Membership

Over half the total number of employees in the Irish Republic belong to trade unions. Though it is not easy to obtain precise data, the latest available total (for 1970) is estimated by the Irish Congress of Trade Unions (ICTU) to be 386 800 — (286 800 men and 100 000 women). Among men the proportion of trade unionists is put at 57 per cent and among women at 40 per cent.

This is a degree of unionization exceeded in the EEC countries only by Belgium and Denmark.

The Irish position is complicated by the existence of unions with head offices outside the Republic and by the fact that some Irish unions organize workers both in the North and in the South, while many British-based unions, although the bulk of their members are in the North, have a foothold in the South. This situation is due to traditional and historical factors. When Ireland was part of Britain, its workers (particularly craft workers) became members of British unions. But the membership of these unions progressively declined as, for political and emotional reasons, the move to Irish-based unions gathered force.

Figure 9:2 shows the trade union membership position, according to the latest available information. Total trade union membership in the Republic increased by 58 800 between 1960 and 1970.

Figure 9:2 shows the extent to which membership is concentrated in a few large unions, the ten which represent about 70 per cent of the total membership, while 85 unions cater for the remaining 30 per cent.

The membership of the largest unions, both in the Republic and the North is shown in Figure 9:3.

Trade unionism is weakest in the agricultural sector and certain service industries. It is strongest in manufacturing industry, public utilities and transport. The growth in the size and influence of non-manual unions, which now account for about a third of total union membership, has been a striking feature of recent years. Organization is particularly developed among bank and insurance workers. Many of the white-collar and professional workers have their own unions.

A Commission on Vocational Organization, which reported during the 1940s, regarded the multiplicity of unions as one of the major weaknesses of the Irish movement and the cause of considerable, and sometimes open, inter-union friction. Despite many attempts to bring about rationalization, the multiplicity has persisted. There are only two fewer unions now than there were in 1960. The small unions, particularly in the civil service and

Figure 9:2 Trade union membership

	Republic	Northern	All Ireland
Number of trade unions	95	77	147
Membership of general			
unions	216 600	103 400	320 000
White-collar	89 600	71 600	161 200
Other	80 600	88 000	168 600
Total membership	386 800	263 000	649 800
Total membership—Men	286 800*	193 500	480 300
as per cent of total	74%	74%	74%
Total membership—Women	100 000*	69 500	169 500
as per cent of total	26%	26%	26%
White-collar members	130 000*	83 000	213 000
as per cent of total	34%	31%	33%
Percentage of employees			
in trade unions			
Men	57%	66%	61%
Women	40%	36%	38%
Total	52%	54%	53%
10 biggest unions	265 000	168 400	
as per cent of total	69%	72%	

*Estimate

Source: Trade union information, Irish Congress of Trade Unions (ICTU) February 1972

craft occupations, have been unwilling to lose their separate identities. There are, for example, no fewer than four Dublin-based organizations catering for customs and excise staff, with a total membership of just over 1000. There is an association of Irish traditional musicians, as well as a professional musicians' organization and the race-course bookmakers' assistants have their own association with 160 members.

In 1971 the government introduced a Trade Union Act to help rationalize the structure and avoid further fragmentation. Under a 1941 Act, it was possible for a group of as few as 7 people to register with the Registrar of Friendly Societies, lodge a deposit with the High Court and thereby obtain a negotiating licence. The new Act imposes stricter conditions for obtaining a licence, such as longer notice, a bigger deposit and a minimum membership of 500. The government has been prepared to give financial help to encourage amalgamations.

Figure 9:3   Membership in the largest unions in the Republic and Northern Ireland

Union	Republic	Northern	All Ireland
Irish Transport & General Workers	150 400	6 400	156 800
Amalgamated Transport and General Workers	18 100	83 200	101 300
Amalgamated Union of Engineering Workers (engineering section)	5 400	27 300	32 700
Workers Union of Ireland	31 000	–	31 000
Electrical/Plumbing	1 700	17 000	18 700
Irish Union of Distributive Workers and Clerks	15 900	–	15 900

Structure

In broad structural terms the Irish trade union movement resembles that of Britain. Unions can be divided into three main groups — occupational, industrial and general, although there is considerable overlapping between the different sections.

Occupational (including *craft*) unions are the oldest type. Entrance has hitherto been via apprenticeship or family tradition, but in recent years, some craft unions have widened the scope of their membership to include semi-skilled workers. Many craft unions have their headquarters in Britain.

Industrial unions are virtually non-existent. Even those which, like the Tailors and Garment Workers or the Shoe and Leather Workers, are concerned specifically with one industry usually operate alongside craft and general unions.

General unions are the predominant form of organization and there are seven of them in the country. They cater mainly for semi-skilled workers and labourers and for skilled workers who do not have to serve a formal apprenticeship. Some also organize clerical and technical workers and employees in the public sector.

The three most important general unions are the Irish TGWU, the British-based Amalgamated TGWU and the Workers' Union of Ireland. Their membership and base of operation is shown in Figure 9:3.

One union, the Irish Women Workers Union, caters exclusively for women in the Republic.

The ITGWU was created in 1909, its main strength being among Dublin's dockworkers. Many Irish patriots, such as Jim Larkin, dissatisfied with remote control from Britain, were determined to break their British links and create an independent Irish organization. The new union was militant, aggressive and patriotic; its leaders played a prominent part in the uprising of 1916. Some Irish patriots were executed and many others were deported.

The union had only about 5000 members at the end of the uprising and its funds were down to £96.

The main credit for its reconstruction must go to its acting general secretary William O'Brien, who rode round the country on his bicycle in search of recruits. He retired only in 1946, having built up a mass membership of well over 100 000.

The patriotic and crusading fervour has persisted down the years. The ITGWU is highly political and has labour members in the Dail and in the new coalition government. Its headquarters are, symbolically, situated in Dublin's most modern and highest skyscraper, the new 'Liberty Hall'.

The ITGWU has aimed to match the efficiency of modern business administration and to provide research, information, education and training facilities. It is organized in six industrial groups:

1   Textiles, laundries, rubber, plastics.

2   Food, drink and tobacco, chemicals, shoe and leather.
3   Building and building materials, public service, forestry.
4   Hospitals, hotels, entertainment, distribution.
5   Transport (rail, road, air), ports and communications.
6   Metal, vehicles, electrical engineering, paper and printing, furniture.

Its general president is Senator Fintan Kennedy and its general secretary is Senator Michael Mullen.

The internal organization of Irish unions varies according to their size and character, and whether they are based in the Republic, the North or in Britain. As shown in Figure 9:4 over four-fifths of the unions in the Republic have head offices in the country.

Figure 9:4   Membership of unions functioning in Ireland

| | Unions with head offices in | | | | | | Total number of union members |
| | Republic | | Northern Ireland | | Britain | | |
	Membership	Percentage of total	Membership	Percentage of total	Membership	Percentage of total	
Republic	332 000	86	–	–	54 800	14	386 000
Northern Ireland	27 900	9	15 400	6	219 700	84	263 000
All Ireland	359 900	55	15 400	2	274 500	42	649 800

Most unions hold annual conferences, which elect an executive council. In most the branch is the basic unit, as in Britain, and the shop steward is usually the union representative on the spot. (The term 'collector' or 'part-time representative' is preferred.) The shop steward is not, however, as influential as his opposite number in Britain. His functions range from the collection of dues to representing the workers *vis-à-vis* the management. In an increasing number of factories, the practice of 'check-off' (deduction of union contributions by the employer) is being applied.

The Irish Congress of Trade unions

Although the broad structure of unions is by tradition similar to that of Great Britain, there are important differences between the central union organizations in the two countries.

The Irish Congress of Trade Unions may lack the resources of the ITGWU and its own headquarters building is unpretentious. Although it has theoretically no power over the affairs of individual unions, the ICTU is in fact in a strong position. It was formed in 1959, as the result of the merger between the Congress of Irish Unions and the Irish Trades Union Congress and covers 96 per cent of all union members in the Republic. The main union outside ICTU is the Irish Bank Officials Association. The ICTU operates on an all-Ireland basis, covering both North and South, and is non-sectarian and non-political. The movement has not been bedevilled by ideological divisions which are a feature of so many European unions, and Communist influence is negligible. All unions with headquarters in Ireland are eligible for affiliation. For those unions with headquarters outside there are special provisions, for example, only Irish residents may attend conferences, hold offices or determine issues which concern Irish interests.

The ICTU lists as its five main objectives:

1 To uphold the democratic character and structure of the trade union movement and the workers' rights to organize and strike.
2 To support democratic government and promote the social and economic policies of the workers of Ireland.
3 To encourage cooperation in national economic activities.
4 To secure for Irish workers 'adequate and effective participation' in the industries where they work.
5 To cooperate with trade unions in other countries.

On a practical level, the ICTU is concerned with the improvement of wages and working conditions. It helps to encourage recruitment and organization; promotes inter-union cooperation, amalgamations and federations; and provides advice and guidance on education, training, research, labour law and kindred subjects. In general, it represents Irish workers in industrial relations and in legislative and administrative matters. Its leaders are regularly consulted by the government and serve on the country's main economic, social and labour advisory bodies.

The ICTU's principal officer is its general secretary, in 1973 Mr Ruaidhri Roberts, with Mr Donal Nevin as assistant general secretary. Congress meets annually to receive the report of its executive council and to debate a very wide range of economic, industrial and political issues. The executive council which is the ICTU's main executive body is elected on the basis of proportional representation in order that there should be no domination by the biggest unions.

There is a disputes committee which adjudicates on such matters as poaching of membership, transfers and inter-union rivalry and operates on lines parallel to the 'Bridlington' agreement in the UK. There is also an appeals board which hears appeals by groups of trade unionists about lack of service by their unions. (Individual members may appeal only in cases of expulsion).

The ICTU appears to wield greater authority over its affiliated members than does the British TUC over its affiliated members. Unions seem more ready to accept its leadership and guidance, and twice since 1970 it has conducted direct national negotiations with the employers which have determined the course of wage movements for the entire country. This development, which is akin to the Scandinavian pattern, is described in the next section.

The ICTU's opposite number on the employers' side is the Federated Union of Employers, which deals with all matters involving labour and social relations. A separate body, the Confederation of Irish Industries, is responsible for commercial and industrial policies.

There are several separate employer bodies for different industries, but the FUE, which has 1713 member companies, is the coordinator and spokesman for employers on labour matters. Its representatives serve jointly with ICTU leaders on many advisory bodies.

Collective Bargaining and Industrial Relations

Voluntary collective bargaining is the basis of wage determination in the Republic. It is recognized as a right and encouraged by the law. The state does not intervene in wage negotiations, except in the case of agricultural workers, whose minimum rates are covered by the Agricultural Wages Act 1936 and fixed by a statutory board. In a number of other industries, where workers are poorly organized, there are joint labour committees, which lay down minimum rates of pay and conditions of employment. There are 23 committees operating in such occupations as hotels, hairdressing, packing, shirt-making and tailoring.

Apart from this, wages are determined by negotiations between employers and unions at industrial, district or company level. Most agreements, as well as covering wages, hours and working conditions, contain procedural clauses setting out arrangements for the settlement of disputes and grievances.

The negotiation in December 1970 of a National Pay Agreement at the National Employer/Labour Conference marked a significant departure from previous practice. It was reached as a result of the government's decision to introduce a Bill to curb incomes and prices. Faced with the threat of state intervention and compulsory wage-fixing, the two sides came to an agreement and the government withdrew its legislation.

The preamble to the Agreement recognized the need for moderation in costs and prices and urged action to increase efficiency and maintain industrial peace. It ran for 18 months in two stages. In the first 12-month stage, it allowed for a £2 a week increase for men, with adjustments to narrow the gap between men's and women's pay, followed by a second 6-month stage, with a 4 per cent increase, plus a cost of living escalator. The Agreement ruled out industrial action in support of claims in excess of these amounts. It also allowed negotiations on claims to remove 'genuine anomalies'. Questions of interpretation of the Agreement were to be referred to the National Employer/Labour Congerence. A second National Pay Agreement was negotiated in July 1972, on very much the same lines, but allowing for somewhat higher increases.

Critics of the Agreements maintained that they were themselves inflationary and allowed too much scope for secondary claims arising out of the 'anomalies' clause. The FUE and the ICTU however held that the alternatives were an uncoordinated round of wage claims, or government intervention, and that it was necessary to have an element of flexibility in the Agreement.

The main responsibility for the settlement of disputes in the Republic rests with the Irish Labour Court, a body set up in 1946 under the Industrial Relations Act. The Court is independent of government, although its members are appointed by the Minister of Labour; it is composed of nominees of the FUE and the ICTU with a neutral chairman and deputy chairman.

The Court's main function is conciliation. It deploys a team of conciliators who help the parties to resolve their disputes. If they are unable to reach agreement, these industrial relations officers will act as mediators at a conciliation conference. They are not arbitrators and do not issue findings or recommendations. About 500 disputes are dealt with by the conciliation service each year and 75-80 per cent of the cases are settled. The conciliators travel all over the country and also help industries and firms to establish viable procedure agreements.

The Labour Court has powers to investigate a dispute if the parties have made a genuine, but unsuccessful effort to reach settlement, and if both sides ask it to. The Court can also initiate an investigation if there are exceptional circumstances, but on the whole it prefers disputes to be settled by conciliation and investigations to be regarded as a last resort.

The Labour Court is not a court of law. Its proceedings are informal and usually held in private. There is no legal obligation on workers or employers to accept its recommendations, though in practice they usually do so.

The Court has other functions. It helps industries to form voluntary joint industrial councils which negotiate on and deal with the problems of specific industries. It also maintains a register of agreements, on a voluntary basis. Disputes not connected with pay or working conditions may be referred to Rights Commissioners who are appointed by the Labour Minister. They make recommendations which become binding if, on appeal, the Labour Court so decided.

Disputes

Despite the industrial peace-keeping machinery, Ireland has been fairly strike-prone. Between 1961 and 1969 an average of 1018 days per 1000 workers was lost in disputes, and Ireland came fourth highest in the ILO's list of 18 countries. The 1970 figure, however, was inflated by the prolonged banking dispute and in 1971 and 1972, as the result of the National Pay Agreement, the number and intensity of strikes diminished.

Figure 9:5 shows the total number of strikes from 1962-1971 and Figure 9:6 shows the individual industries affected by strikes in 1968-1971. The estimated figure for 1972 is 218 340 working days lost.

The most vulnerable areas, as in the UK, are transport and engineering, and the two major causes of disputes are wages and questions of engagement and dismissal.

Many strikes last for a considerable period, and though there is no social assistance for strikers' families, unions almost invariably provide strike benefit.

The Balance Sheet

How far have the Irish unions succeeded in their aim of raising the standard of living of their members? This question can best be answered by examining the annual trend of earnings and prices in recent years (see Figure 9:7). It shows that money earnings outstripped price increases and productivity, but that the level of real earnings fell far short of that of money earnings and has continued to do so. According to the OECD survey of Ireland (March 1973) prices during 1972 increased faster in Ireland than in any of the major OECD countries, averaging 8½ per cent above the 1971 level.

Money earnings increased rapidly during 1970-1973. Men's average weekly earnings in manufacture were £24.00 in 1970, £27.11 in 1971 and £30.98 in

Figure 9:5   Industrial disputes in Ireland

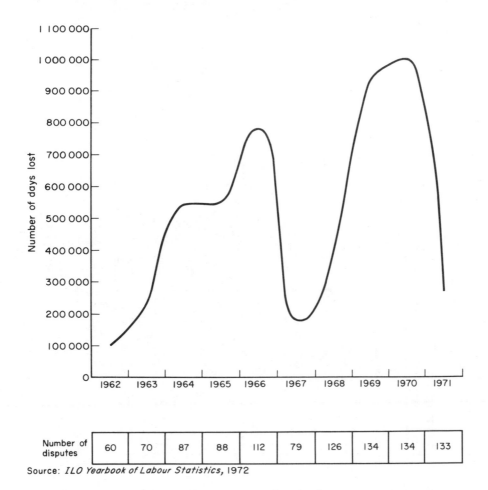

| Number of disputes | 60 | 70 | 87 | 88 | 112 | 79 | 126 | 134 | 134 | 133 |

Source: *ILO Yearbook of Labour Statistics*, 1972

1972, while the number of hours worked dropped from 45.2 to 44.8.

The gap between men's and women's rates is still very wide. Women's weekly earnings in manufacturing averaged £15.08 in late 1972, but their working hours were considerably shorter. One-third of the workers in manufacturing industry are women but relatively few married women go out to work. They tend to have large families and there is a lack of child care facilities. In 1970 the government appointed a Commission to enquire into the status of women. In an interim report, the Commission recommended the introduction of equal pay by stages for men and women doing the same work, or work judged to be of equal value. Specific provision was made in

Figure 9:6   Industrial disputes within industries 1968-71

Industrial group	Disputes which began during year				Workpeople involved				Man-days lost			
	1968	1969	1970	1971	1968	1969	1970	1971	1968	1969	1970	1971
Agriculture	1	–	1	–	34	–	5	–	204	–	20	–
Mining	9	9	8	5	5 267	3 114	876	1 000	135 884	40 543	21 019	15 366
Food drink and tobacco	8	7	8	10	657	740	572	2 823	3 280	2 545	1 411	28 092
Textiles and clothing	8	10	10	9	2 320	1 201	993	2 889	11 235	5 994	6 194	7 400
Woodworking	7	–	6	7	554	–	312	817	819	–	2 301	3 821
Paper and print	–	3	–	2	–	128	–	43	–	1 314	–	71
Chemicals	3	4	–	3	566	1 578	–	329	2 405	15 531	–	13 315
Clay, glass, cement	2	5	4	4	506	1 057	1 117	556	1 098	8 171	88 779	1 803
Metals and engineering	25	22	25	18	3 909	6 017	3 275	5 631	42 983	32 087	18 568	80 298
Other manufacturing	5	5	8	7	1 671	415	822	1 390	15 757	2 818	3 096	5 488
Building	18	19	14	20	6 876	1 395	743	3 725	75 399	10 127	7 581	14 053
Electricity, gas	5	11	8	6	6 368	2 429	1 309	1 070	22 015	30 253	7 706	6 572
Commerce	11	19	20	14	900	2 329	7 082	763	25 253	25 211	791 128	15 101
Transport	12	10	15	15	4 461	2 105	2 618	17 621	9 680	7 066	33 154	59 093
Services	9	8	7	13	4 791	7 362	5 968	5 126	59 674	125 392	45 757	23 297
Maintenance	–	1	–	–	–	3 890	–	–	–	628 848	–	–
TOTAL	126	123	134	133	38 880	61 760	28 752	43 783	405 686	935 900	1 007 714	273 770

Source: *Irish Statistical Bulletin*, March 1972

the second National Pay Agreement for the introduction of the first stage of equal pay.

The Irish system of determining conditions of employment is similar to that in Britain. Social security contributions and benefits are on a flat-rate basis, though pay-related benefits are due to come into operation in April 1974. Benefits are below the levels of the original EEC countries, though the 1973 Budget raised some welfare benefits very considerably. The flat-rate benefits approximate to those in the United Kingdom.

Generally terms and conditions of employment, hours, holidays etc. are arranged through direct collective bargaining. A maximum working week of

Figure 9:7(a)   Percentage increases in weekly earnings of industrial workers and in consumer prices 1963-71

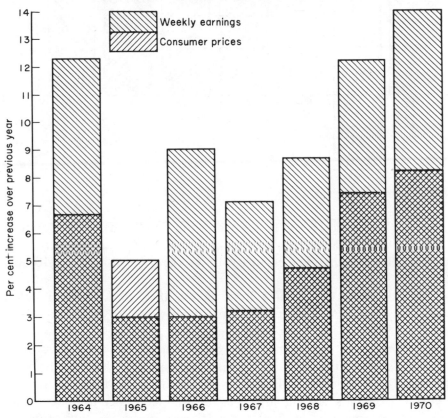

Source: ICTU Information, February 1972

Figure 9:7(b)   Percentage increases in real earnings and in GNP per person at work 1963-71

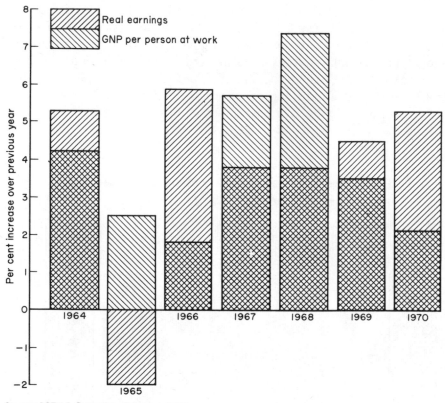

Source: ICTU Information, February 1972

48 hours for those over 18 was laid down in the Conditions of Employment Act 1936, but under collective agreement the length of the working week varies from 40-42 hours. The majority of workers are now on a 40-hour week.

The official amount of annual leave is set at 2 weeks plus 6 public holidays, but collective agreements usually provide for an extra week's holiday.

Overtime rates are determined by direct negotiation and vary from industry to industry; in many cases the rate for manual workers is time and a half for the first 6-8 hours, followed by double time, with special rates at holidays and weekends. An employer has to obtain a licence to operate shift working and observe certain limitations (for example, no shift must be longer than 9 hours, periods of 15 minutes rest between 3-4 hours and there are limitations on women's shift work.)

Workers who become redundant are entitled to a lump sum payment under the Redundancy Payments Acts of 1967 and 1971 after 2 years or more service. There are also weekly redundancy payments according to length of service. The employer contributes 10p per week for men and women employees to a redundancy fund. Disputes are dealt with by a special redundancy appeals tribunal.

Cooperation

As in most European countries, the Irish trade unionists are coming to think increasingly in terms of extending their influence on the shopfloor and exercising a voice in industrial affairs.

At national level there is provision for consultation on all aspects of employment and industrial relations through the National Employer/Labour Conference. This includes representatives of the employers in the public and private sectors, and the Irish Congress of Trade Unions, and, as already indicated, has come to play an increasingly important part in national negotiations.

There is no legislation establishing consultative machinery in industry, but committees have been set up in a number of industries and companies, where they usually take the form of works councils. In addition, many firms have joint safety committees. There has, apparently been no great enthusiasm among the workers for formal consultation or industrial democracy. There is little evidence of profit-sharing schemes in industry.

The Irish system of industrial relations is a blend of the voluntary and statutory, with the emphasis on voluntary settlement.

Both sides of industry resent government interference and prefer to settle their own affairs directly as shown by the establishment of the National Employer/Labour Conference. The role of government is seen primarily as setting the general climate and atmosphere and taking measures to encourage productivity and training, as well as, by legislation, to protect and safeguard the less well-paid sections.

The government, however, consults the two sides of industry through the FUE and the ICTU on every aspect of its economic and social policy and its representatives serve on a wide range of advisory bodies. The Irish unions have cooperated in all the relevant institutions and, under wise leadership, have played a vital part in the postwar development of their country and in raising it from a backward agricultural economy to a modern industrial society.

10

Italy

Economic Background

Italy is the second largest country in the EEC in terms of area (301,200 square kilometres) and third largest in terms of population (54½ million). Its population density at 179 inhabitants per square kilometre is just above the EEC average.

Rome, the capital, has a population of about 2.8 million. The major urban concentrations are in the north, based on the industrial cities of Milan (1.7 million), Turin (1.2 million) and the port of Genoa (845 000). In the south, Naples is the largest city with 1.3 million inhabitants. Palermo, in Sicily, has a population of 700 000. Other important cities include Bologna (484 000), Florence (455 000), Venice (366 000) and Trieste (281 000).

Employment

The labour force totals about 19 million, of whom 3.6 million work in agriculture and 8.2 million in industry. The proportion employed in agriculture has steadily declined — from about 35 per cent in 1958 to about 20 per cent in the 1970s.

Industry is concentrated in the north, which is the most densely populated and prosperous part of the country. In the south agriculture predominates and there is high unemployment and widespread poverty. This has led to mass emigration to the north and to other parts of Europe.

Efforts have been made by successive governments to aid the under-developed areas of the south. Capital grants, loans, tax reliefs and a variety of other forms of assistance are available to firms prepared to develop in the Mezzogiorno area and priority for southern development was laid down in a Law of October 1971.

Figure 10:1   Analysis of employment by principal sectors

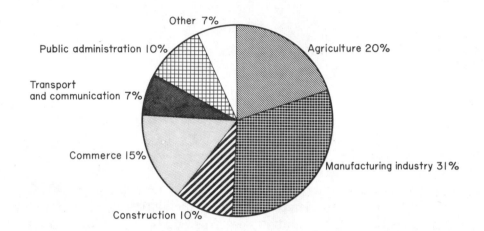

The most rapidly developing industrial sectors include steel, chemicals and petro-chemicals, pharmaceuticals, textiles, motor vehicles, mechanical and electrical engineering and paper production.

Two state corporations have been set up to supervise and control various industries, including steel, shipbuilding, mechanical engineering, telecommunications, sea and air transport, hydrocarbons and petroleum.

Tourism plays an important part in Italy's balance of payments.

The Economy

Industrial development came relatively late in Italy, which did not itself become a united nation until 1870. Since 1950 the economic growth has been extremely rapid — increasing by nearly 400 per cent between 1950 and 1970, by when the GNP had reached £37 280 million. The growth rate was 4.7 per cent in 1969 and was expected to be 5 per cent during 1973.

Exports account for about one quarter of the GNP. Italy's trading partners are the other EEC countries, led by West Germany and France.

Population density in principal regions

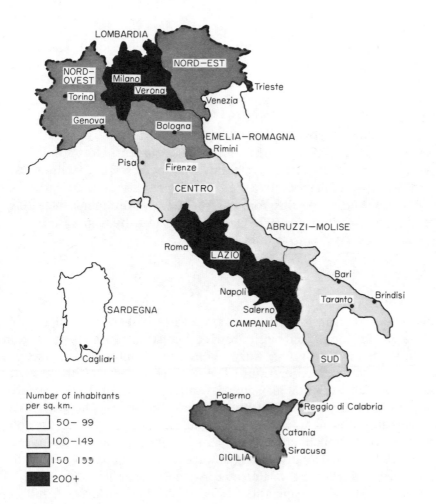

LOMBARDIA

NORD–EST

NORD–OVEST

Milano

Verona

Trieste

Torino

Venezia

Genova

Bologna

EMELIA–ROMAGNA

Rimini

Pisa

Firenze

CENTRO

ABRUZZI–MOLISE

Roma

LAZIO

Bari

Napoli

Taranto

Brindisi

Salerno

CAMPANIA

SARDEGNA

SUD

Cagliari

Palermo

Reggio di Calabria

Number of inhabitants
per sq. km.

Catania

Siracusa

	50– 99
	100–149
	150 199
	200+

SICILIA

Many firms in Italy, particularly in the food sector, are owned by foreign companies.

Government

Italy became a Republic in 1948, and is headed by a President, elected by the two chambers for a 7-year period. These two chambers are the Chamber of Deputies and the Senate, both elected on the basis of proportional representation. The President nominates the Council of Ministers led by the Prime Minister.

The Italian system of government was established in the Constitution of 1948. Ever since, there has been instability in government. Most administrations have been coalitions, with or without the Socialist groups, under the domination of Christian-democrats. In 1972 a Conservative coalition headed by Signor Giulio Andreotti, was formed (the 34th government since Italy became a Republic). It fell in 1973 and was replaced by a more left-wing coalition under Signor Mariano Rumor.

Membership

The Italian trade union movement dates from the middle of the last century and its development coincided with growing industrialization, especially in the north. By the turn of the century about half a million workers were organized in 27 national federations. The various organizations came together in the socialist-orientated General Confederation of Labour (CGL) which sought to acquire a central authority over its affiliates. The progress of the Confederation was hampered by the parallel growth of the Catholic Workers' movement, which grew rapidly in Piedmont, Venice, Lombardy and Sicily, and was particularly strong among textile workers. In 1917 the Catholic Confederation (CIL) was created, with 20 national unions and 26 provincial and regional organizations. By 1920 it had over 1 million members, compared with the CGL's 2.2 million. The Catholics rejected the concept of the class struggle and accepted that of cooperation within the capitalist society.

During the long years of the Mussolini regime, unions were merged into the corporate state and it was not until after the Liberation that free organizations could emerge. As in Germany, the task of reconstruction had to be tackled from scratch. Under the Rome Pact of June 1944, it was agreed to set up a unified body, the Italian General Confederation of Labour

(CGIL), embracing Communist, Socialist and Christian-democrat faiths. The agreement was contained in a lofty 'Declaration on the achievement of trade union unity', but it was to prove short-lived. Internal political and religious tensions were too strong and the movement split in several directions. The Christian-democrats, together with the minority Socialist and Republican groups formed a new alliance in 1948, leaving the Communists in control of the Confederation.

Later the Socialists and Republicans withdrew and formed their own centre, the Italian Federation of Labour (FIL). This was followed by the secession of the Social-democrats to form a new group, the Italian Union of Labour (UIL).

This brief description of the chequered and confusing history of union development is necessary to an understanding of the present position in Italy. Largely as a result of the internal divisions, the percentage of workers who belong to unions is probably only about 35-40 per cent of the labour force, which is estimated to be about 19 million.

The unions themselves place the proportion at about 50 per cent, but this is probably exaggerated.

The main organizations in Italy (1973) are:

1   The Italian General Confederation of Labour (CGIL), set up in 1944, and claiming about 4 million members. It is affiliated to the Communist-dominated World Federation of Trade Unions.
2   The Italian Confederation of Labour Unions (CISL) formed in 1950 as a result of defections from the CGIL. It is affiliated to the International Confederation of Free Trade Unions.
3   The Italian Union of Labour (UIL) also formed in 1950 and close to the Socialist and Republican parties. It claims about 800 000 members, and is also affiliated to the ICFTU.
4   The Christian Association of Italian Workers (ACLI) is a radical social and religious organization, with about 600 000 members.
5   The Italian Confederation of National Workers Unions (CISNAL) formed in 1950 by neo-fascist and monarchist groups. It claims a membership of 76 000. It has no international affiliations and has no relationships with any of the other confederations.

The main seat of union power lies in the industrial north, and organization is weak in the under-developed regions of the south. Membership is highest among metal workers, probably about 70 per cent, and lowest among white-collar and service workers.

The relatively low level of organization is attributable to the divisions within the movement but recent movements towards unification could stimulate recruitment. The uprising in France in May 1968 contributed to the growing strength of the militants in Italy, and to the emergence of a younger and more sophisticated generation of trade unionists. Despite ideological differences at the top, workers' representatives within the plants adopted a common front against the employers in pressing for improved wages and working conditions. As in other countries the metalworkers set the pace, and pressure from below stimulated progress towards unification.

The movement reached crisis-point in the so-called 'hot autumn' of 1969, when the country was engulfed in a tidal wave of strikes, involving about 5 million workers.

All the main union centres were involved and came together to develop a new strategy.

The CGIL, although Communist-led, has always pronounced its independence from Moscow — the Italians have developed their own brand of Communism — and led the move to seek alliances with other groups. It seems prepared to modify its revolutionary principles in an effort to achieve central-left solidarity, concentrating on broad social and economic objectives such as employment, housing, health, pensions, education and other areas of reform.

In 1969-70, at their respective conferences, all three union bodies adopted resolutions which effectively severed their links with the main political parties and thus opened the road to independent and united union action. Even the Christian unions, which in other EEC countries have bitterly opposed any links with the Communist-led unions, carried a motion urging 'the necessity of making the aim of organic unity a reality in concrete terms as rapidly as possible'. The Social-democrat UIL stressed the need to eliminate 'misery, unemployment, illiteracy and other social evils'.

Despite a number of hurdles still to be overcome (for example, the question of international affiliation) and opposition from some sections of the Christians and the UIL, complete unification is hoped for by the mid-1970s. The trend has been strengthened by the fact that employers in the private sector are centralized in the associations attached to Confindustria, the General Confederation of Italian Industry. This body contains 105 area and 98 national associations and represents the vast majority of private employers. In the industries in which the state participates or owns, there is a separate body Intersind, which negotiates independently with the unions.

Intersind negotiates in iron and steel, shipping, air transport, telephones, radio and TV, chemicals, petroleum and textile industries.

The trend towards unification is by far the most important feature of the modern Italian labour scene.

Structure

All the three main national centres, CGIL, CISL and UIL follow the same structural pattern. Unions are grouped vertically according to industry and trade, and there are horizontal regional and branch structures. These come together in chambers of labour.

At factory level, workers are represented by elected 'delegates' (shop stewards). Their effectiveness varies from industry to industry. They are strongest in textiles, clothing, rubber and in metalworking, where it is estimated that there are more than 22 000 delegates belonging to 1400 factory committees. At Fiat works, all metalworkers belong to a single Federation, the FLM.

Collective Bargaining and Industrial Relations

In most Italian industries, voluntary collective contracts cover wages and working conditions. These are generally regarded as setting standards for the entire industry, although they bind only members of the organizations that sign the contract. It is the task of Ministry of Labour officials to make sure that no worker receives wages which are inferior to those established in the collective contract.

Contracts are usually industry-based and cover both salaried and manual workers. They define employment conditions, categories of skill, minimum rates of pay, hours and holidays. Agreements contain a cost of living escalation clause, adjusted at quarterly intervals. The tendency is for the conclusion of long-term contracts, usually 3-4 years. Bargains reached between the unions and the state holding companies usually set the pattern for private companies, and bargains with larger companies set the pattern for smaller firms.

Originally, collective negotiations were highly centralized, but during the late 1960s, and particularly after the autumn of 1969, there was a rapid development of plant bargaining. In the metalworking industry, an agreement with the state-controlled concerns provided that national contracts could be supplemented by plant-level agreements dealing with such matters as piece-rates, job classification and output bonuses. This system was called 'articulated bargaining' and spread throughout industry. After 1969 workers' representatives at shopfloor level played a much more direct part in negotiations than formerly, when this had been largely left to union officials. It has been estimated that in 1970/1 some 4400 plant agreements covering more than 1½ million workers were in force. Most deal with local wage increases, piece-rates, bonuses and incentive payments, or with grading systems, hours and arrangements for introducing a shorter working week.

An important point at issue is the upgrading of skills and the 'degradation' of the assembly line. At Fiat, for example, a new 3-year contract provides for a drastic reduction in the number of grades, with the elimination of the lower grades and a form of job enrichment, with the emphasis on team productivity incentive bonuses.

The Fiat negotiations were characterized by tough bargaining and a protracted labour dispute which resulted in the employers meeting most of the men's points, after the invervention of the Minister of Labour.

Similarly an important agreement in the chemical industry (March 1973) resulted in the restructuring of jobs, the reduction of grades and the introduction of flexible working time.

The Ministry of Labour and Social Security provides mediation and conciliation services, locally or nationally. Either party can call on its officers in the event of disagreement, or the two parties may agree to set up voluntary arbitration committees.

Any individual worker who has a grievance about his contract can take the matter up with his employer, who should reply within a week. If the worker has not received a reply by then, he can take it up through the works committee, and in the event of continued disagreement, the complaint can be referred to the section of the court dealing with labour matters. Controversies over the interpretation of collective contracts are normally referred to a permanent national commission.

Disputes

Despite this machinery, the Italians are more strike-prone than any other EEC nationals (see Figure 10:2). Italy headed the list of European countries in terms of days lost through strikes during the 1960s, averaging over 1000 per 1000 workers. In the autumn of 1969, 520 million working hours were lost. In 1972, however, Italy's record was surpassed by that of Great Britain, which lost 1542 working days per 1000 workers, compared with Italy's 1410.

Because the unions are not wealthy, few strikes last long and the lightning or 'articulated' strike, aimed to hit where it will hurt most, is favoured. In car plants, for example, key workers on the assembly line take 1-2 hours off by rota, thus disrupting production and causing men to be sent home. Another form of stoppage is the general strike, lasting one day or longer, and usually involving workers in the public sector, for example, railways and postal services. There is no distinction between official and unofficial strikes.

The right to strike is recognized under the Italian Constitution. Italian civil servants are allowed to strike unlike those in many EEC countries.

Some unions are taking actions to limit the incidence of strikes which are increasingly alienating public opinion and damaging their own 'image'.

The Balance Sheet

Despite the divisions in the trade union movement, Italian workers have been able to gain substantial advances in their pay and conditions. In some respects, for example, holidays and fringe benefits, they are the best-off in Europe, even though their level of wages and their standard of living are lower.

They are protected by an elaborate network of labour legislation, covering minimum wages, rest-days, holidays, hours, engagement, length of notice, severance pay, redundancy compensation, as well as social insurance and safety and welfare within the plant.

Fringe benefits are high. The main burden falls on the employer and it has been estimated that the cost of fringe benefits and compulsory social charges amounts to about 85-90 per cent of basic pay.

A bonus is paid for a thirteenth month and there are additional bonuses in respect of housing, transport, clothing, and dirty or dangerous work. Many companies operate welfare schemes for their employees, such as holiday and sports clubs, health and hospital facilities.

A recent concession, as in France, has been the extension to manual workers of monthly status resulting in a growing parity of conditions as between white-collar and blue-collar workers.

The gap between men's and women's earnings narrowed more noticeably in Italy than in many other EEC countries, as a result of accelerating the rate of increase in women's pay. In metalworking, the women's percentage of men's earnings is between 83 and 88 per cent.

Italian workers enjoy long holidays. The minimum laid down by collective agreement is 13-21 days, and there are 17 public holidays, making a total of 30-38 days. Long service workers can receive extra leave. A recent tendency has been to lump some of the public holidays together as part of summer leave, in order to avoid disrupting production.

The standard working week, also determined by collective bargaining, is 40-42 hours. The unions have pressed for the immediate realization of the 40-hour week, and this is now provided in most collective contracts. Unions are anxious to reduce or eliminate overtime.

The movement of prices and earnings since 1969 is shown in Figure 10:3. According to OECD forecasts, hourly earnings were expected to increase by about 18 per cent in 1973 compared with 25 per cent in 1970, while consumer prices were expected to increase by about 7 per cent per annum. In other words the 1973 rounds of wage negotiations were expected to show a considerable slowing down compared with those of 1970.

Figure 10:2   Industrial disputes in Italy

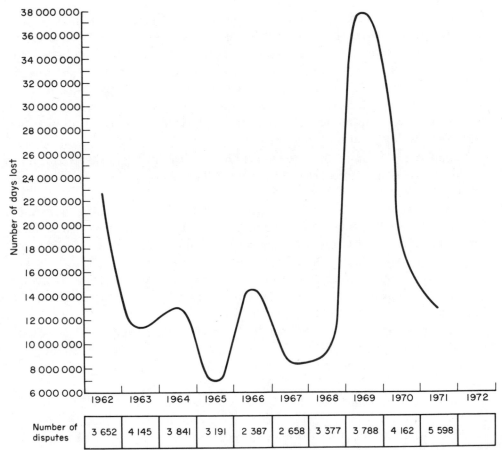

	1962	1963	1964	1965	1966	1967	1968	1969	1970	1971	1972
Number of disputes	3 652	4 145	3 841	3 191	2 387	2 658	3 377	3 788	4 162	5 598	

Source: *ILO Yearbook of Labour Statistics,* 1972

Figure 10:3   Movement of prices and incomes since 1969 (1966 = 100)

	1969	1970	1971	1972 (second quarter)
Price index*	106.2	111.6	105.0	109.6
Hourly earnings				
Agriculture	127.2	149.4	169.9	177.4
Industry	117.0	141.2	158.0	159.5
Transport	111.3	126.4	141.3	145.2
Commerce	113.2	128.1	142.8	148.8
Minimum salaries				
Industry	113.9	130.0	142.8	147.6
Commerce	113.3	126.7	139.0	146.6
Public administration	108.8	111.9	122.3	121.2

*Workers' families, covers food, clothing and housing
Source: *OECD Report on Italy,* November 1972

Labour costs in Italy are higher than in France or the UK. An example of the increasing trend can be seen from the Figure 10:4 of average cost per 1000 workers in metalworking.

Figure 10:4 Average labour cost per 1000 workers in metalworking

	Lire	Index
October 1971	1 928 39	100
March 1972	1 975 54	108.4
October 1972	2 025 53	110.3

Source: Unione Industriale di Torino

In general, Italian unions are in favour of reducing the differential between the pay of skilled and unskilled workers.

Cooperation

A very important development from the union point of view was the passage
of an Act in May 1970, incorporating the 'Workers' Charter'. This charter was
originally launched in the 1950s, as a means of guaranteeing workers' civil
and organizational rights at their place of work, and bringing pressure to bear
on employers who still refused to recognize unions. The Act, which was
piloted through by a Socialist Minister of Labour, prohibits employers from
discriminating against workers on the grounds of union membership and
encourages the system of union delegates at company level. It grants
increased authority to works committees, for example, it bars the use of
audiovisual apparatus as means of production control without the consent of
the committee. Employers may not discipline a worker without giving him
the chance of stating his case in the presence of a union representative. They
must provide the works committee with a meeting place and allow it to meet
within working hours.

Works committees or councils have been set up in firms employing more
than 40 workers, under a voluntary agreement which lays down the
procedure for their operation. The job of these councils is to check the
implementations of contracts, supervise safety and health measures, sort out
individual or collective grievances and advise on matters affecting social
services, sports clubs, etc.

Works council members are elected for 2 years, on the basis of proportional representation. All workers in a plant are entitled to vote.
Membership varies according to the size of the factory, with a maximum of
21 for factories with over 40 000 employees. Candidates usually are
members of a union. Members enjoy a high degree of job security.

The left-wing unions have not been very enthusiastic about works
councils, regarding them as a form of paternalism without any real power,
and preferring to concentrate on increasing the influence of workers'
delegates. But both leaders and rank and file are coming to realize the
potential of the 'consiglio di fabrica' as a means of increasing industrial
democracy.

Despite the widespread use of the strike weapon, relations between
managements and workers are reasonably smooth. The more militant unions
have as their slogan 'permanent conflict', but whatever the long-term aim,
many leaders are realizing the need for cooperation in the interests of the
Italian economy and social reform. The two sides of industry are represented
on the National Economic and Labour Council which advises the government on labour legislation. The unions cooperate in encouraging training and

upgrading, which is often the subject of a clause in the collective contract (for example, in printing, in contracts with Olivetti and Siemens, and with the state holding bodies). They have also been pressing for a more vigorous policy for the development of backward areas. For example, Fiat workers agreed in 1970 to spread the cut in working hours over a longer period in return for a guarantee by the company that it would invest in the Mezzogiorno, the impoverished south.

The Italian government plays an extremely important part in industrial relations and, as has been shown, there is legislation covering almost every aspect of labour activities. Since 1969 the three confederations have tended to deal directly with the government, particularly on matters of social reform and unemployment. The government operated a national development plan, with the emphasis on helping the regions, but in the first four years (1966-70), performance fell short of promise, and northern expansion continued at the expense of the south. Hopes were expressed that the new government elected in 1973 would pursue regional policies more vigorously and effectively, as well as speeding progress in social reform, such as housing, health and education.

11

Luxembourg

Economic Background

Luxembourg is the smallest country in the EEC, in terms of both population and area. The Grand Duchy covers an area of about 2600 square kilometres, and is only 82 kilometres from north to south and 57 kilometres from east to west. Its total population is 345 000, and its density 131 per square kilometre. The capital city of Luxembourg has a population of just over 75 000.

Most people are bilingual and French and German are the official languages. Local people speak Luxembourgeois.

Luxembourg is an important EEC centre and many of the Community's economic and financial institutions are situated there.

Employment

About half the total employed population of 150 000 work in industry. Steel is the principal sector and employs about 50 per cent of the industrial labour force. Other manufacturing sectors include growth industries such as chemicals, plastics, rubbers and tyres. Goodyear, established in 1951, is now the second largest enterprise in the country.

Agriculture and forestry employ 10 per cent of the labour force. Wine is produced in the south and tourism is an important revenue producer.

Luxembourg has experienced full employment since the end of the Second World War. About a quarter of its working population come from other, mainly EEC, countries.

Figure 11:1   Analysis of employment by principal sectors

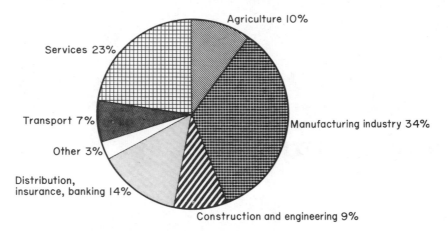

The Economy

The GNP was £435 000 in 1971 derived mainly from industry. The steel industry contributes 25 per cent of the GNP and nearly 70 per cent of exports. The reliance on steel resulted in a relatively slow growth rate, but Luxembourg has the highest level of per capita income of any EEC member. The encouragement of growth industries is expected to lead to a higher growth rate in the next decade.

Since the end of the Second World War, the Grand Duchy has developed into an important international financial centre.

West Germany is Luxembourg's principal trading partner, accounting for 40 per cent of its imports and 30 per cent of its exports. Belgium follows with 31 per cent of imports and 22 per cent of exports.

Government

Luxembourg is a constitutional monarchy, with a hereditary prince as head of state. Executive power is exercised by the Council of Ministers. The principal legislature is the 56-member Chamber of Deputies, elected for a period of 5 years. The Council of State (21 members) scrutinizes bills submitted by the Chamber.

Since the end of the Second World War, governments have been based on coalitions of three main parties, with the Social Christians as the largest single force. The current coalition (winter 1973) consists of Social Christians and Democrats, and is generally regarded as centrist. The present Prime Minister is M. Pierre Werner.

Membership and Structure

The Grand Duchy of Luxembourg is a small country, with 345 000 inhabitants. About one-third of the population (147 600) are actively employed. Yet, as in neighbouring Belgium, the trade union movement is characterized by pluralism. It is divided between two main centres which represent the Socialist and Christian viewpoints respectively. Until recently, there was a third (Communist) centre.

Trade unions were first formed in the 1860s and, curiously enough, the first Luxembourg union was founded by Bavarian brewery workers as a local section of the German 'Brauerei Arbeiter Verband'. This was followed by the organization of printers, cigar-makers and glove-makers, but until the twentieth century, trade unions were repressed and counted fewer than 1000 members. The movement remained on a craft basis until the First World War, when powerful unions representing miners, steel workers and textile workers began to emerge. They grouped themselves into a General Confederation of Labour (CGT) and between 1917 and 1920, union membership rose from 8000 to 26 000. The CGT was militant and Socialist in character and launched a series of strikes and factory 'sit-ins' at the end of the First World War.

Hopes of a united movement were short-lived, for in 1920 the Christians revived their separate organization which had originally been set up in 1906 but lapsed during the First World War.

Trade union membership represents about 50 per cent of the labour force. The main centres at the present time are:

1   The Confédération générale du travail (CGT), Socialist-oriented, affiliated to the ICFTU, with a membership of 30 000.
2   The Confédération luxembourgeoise des syndicats chrétiens (CLSC), with 13 500 claimed members.

The Communist organization, Freie Letzeburger Arbechterverband (FLA) was dissolved in the mid-1960s and its members were absorbed into the CGT.

In addition there are a number of organizations, catering for specific interests and without political or religious affiliations. The Independent Union of Artisans (NHV), and the Federation of Private Sector Employees (FEP) as well as unions for central and local government employees. Their total membership is about 10 000.

Luxembourg has proportionately more foreign workers than any other

EEC country, amounting to about one-third of the total labour force. They are eligible for membership of unions and of works and union committees.

The CGT is divided into two main sections — the Federation of Luxembourg Workers (LAV) which organizes workers in mining, iron and steel, building, chemicals, textiles and consumer industries, such as leather, pottery, food, drink and tobacco, and the National Federation of Railwaymen, Transport Workers, Civil Servants and Employees (FNCTTFEL).

The CGT, according to its consititution, is anti-capitalist. It declares:

> The ultimate aim of trade union activity is the transformation of the present society into a classless society where social justice rules and where labour, creator of all values, will be considered as a fundamental factor and where the workers will be able to live without social fear.

One of its main objectives is the extension of workers' participation on the boards of companies.

The CLSC's philosophy is based on Christian social doctrines laid down in Papal encyclicals. It believes in cooperation with private enterprise and is opposed to the extension of nationalization.

Both main bodies have centralized structures, the Christians even more than the Socialists. Union organization, as in Belgium, is partly vertical (with local sections) and partly horizontal (with industrial federations).

Since mining and steel account for 25 per cent of the Grand Duchy's GNP and 50 per cent of its employment, it is inevitable that the trade union movement should be dominated by the unions in these sectors. Recent efforts have, however, been made, to diversify the economy by attracting foreign (largely American) investment in chemicals, tyre production, artificial fibres, tobacco and metal-processing. There has also been an explosive growth in banking. The number of employees in banks increased from 2223 in 1966 to 3706 in 1970. Luxembourg, as the headquarters of many EEC institutions, has a large population of international civil servants.

Despite their ideological differences, the main confederations work together in practice and have established a common action committee which presents their views to the employers and the government, on such issues as wages, prices, economic planning, hours of work and holidays and social security. On social issues they are in broad agreement.

In recent elections of works delegates in iron and steel committees, the CGT organization LAV had 70.4 per cent of the votes, compared with 22.4 per cent for the Christians. In small- and medium-sized enterprises and public services, the Christians did rather better with 31 per cent compared with the CGT's 60.2 per cent.

None of the three confederations has a civil status in law. Only in 1936 did they acquire the full right to freedom of association and the right to strike.

The chief employers organization is the Fédération des industriels luxembourgeois.

Collective Bargaining and Industrial Relations

Minimum wage rates are fixed by law, and wages are linked with the cost of living. The main basis for wage determination is the collective contract negotiated, as in Belgium, by joint management-labour bodies. These include the 'most representative' organizations, that is, in practice the CGT and the Christians. Once a collective contract has been signed and approved, the government usually extends its application over the whole of the industry concerned.

A contract remains in force unless it has been denounced by either party three months before its expiration or the conclusion of a new contract. The procedure for concluding collective contracts is laid down by law and strikes and lock-outs are illegal until the procedure has been followed.

The machinery for dealing with industrial disputes is laid down by the parties themselves. The government operates a conciliation service and can act without an invitation but its decisions are not imposed.

Arbitration is not compulsory, though both parties may agree to voluntary arbitration. Labour courts deal with any disputes over the interpretation of contracts.

Disputes

Luxembourg workers have the right to strike, although it is circumscribed under the official procedure. Because of this, and because most collective contracts contain a 'social peace' clause, the incidence of disputes is very low. The Grand Duchy has long enjoyed a reputation for stability and by temperament and tradition, the majority of the workers – in spite of the militant terms of the CGT constitution – are conservative and in favour of industrial peace. (Their dislike of change is shown in the fact that one of their favourite songs is called 'We want to stay as we are'.) The stability was threatened early in 1973 by the threat of a strike over a new wage agreement in the steel industry. This would have been the first strike since 1953 and the second since 1945. But in the end, agreement was reached through the conciliation procedure. Luxembourg has remained strike-free.

The Balance Sheet

The Grand Duchy is prosperous and enjoys the highest per capita income of any EEC country. There is no unemployment and large numbers of foreign workers have been recruited to offset the national labour shortage. Despite their relatively strong organization, it cannot be said that the high standard of living derives mainly from union pressure. It is rather, the result of the exploitation of mineral resources and the growth of foreign investment and financial institutions.

The general rate of wage increase during the 1960s was slower than in other EEC countries. The highest paid groups are ore-mining and processing, iron and steel, metal manufacturing, printing, fibres, rubber and plastic, non-ferrous metals and non-metallic mining.

The statutory working working week is 48 hours for manual workers and 44 for clerical workers, but under collective agreements, its length has been progressively reduced. Thus the miners and steel workers have a 40-hour week and most other industries work a 43/44 hour week. Permission to exceed the legal maximum must be obtained from the Labour Inspectorate. There is relatively little overtime worked.

Luxembourg workers are entitled to 16½ days annual paid leave, with additional days based on age and length of service, and 10 public holidays. Youths under 18 receive an extra 6½ days.

There is a comprehensive social security scheme, covering health, workmen's compensation, old age, sickness and family allowances, and public assistance. Benefits are wage-related and are on a generous scale.

Cooperation

The absence of strikes reflects the calm state of industrial relations in the Grand Duchy. Unions and employers participate in many official committees and organizations, for example, the Social Security Office, the National Labour Office, the Office for Higher Productivity and the Economic and Social Council. There is also a system of 'chambres professionnelles', which are elected consultative bodies that advise the government and parliament on all aspects of labour legislation. There are six such chambers, covering employers, clerical workers, manual workers, artisans, civil servants and farmers.

At local level, there is a system of works councils which are compulsory in any enterprise with more than 12 workers. Elections take place every 4 years. Members are elected by all employees, whether or not they belong to unions. Their functions are mainly advisory, and they are consulted on such matters as training, health and safety, works rules, social security and the arrangement of working hours. Members may not be dismissed while serving on the committee.

12

Netherlands

Economic Background

The Netherlands has a population of just over 13 million. With a land area, much of it below sea level, of only 34 000 square kilometres, its population density at 360 inhabitants per square kilometre is among the highest in the world. Population growth is high and is expected to reach 14.5 million by 1980.

The three largest cities are situated close together in a narrow congested strip in the western part of the country. They are Amsterdam (840 000), Rotterdam (699 000) and The Hague (564 000). The only other city with over a quarter of a million inhabitants is Utrecht with 278 000. A number of smaller towns, with populations of over 100 000, include Eindhoven, Haarlem, Groningen, Tilburg and Nijmegen.

Employment

About 4.7 million people are gainfully employed, 3.7 million men and 1 million women. The Netherlands has the largest services sector of any EEC country. Banking, insurance and shipping provide a substantial foreign exchange revenue.

Industry has developed rapidly since the Second World War, particularly in the field of electronics and chemicals. Several multinational concerns, such as Philips and Royal Dutch/Shell, are based in Holland. Agriculture employs only 7 per cent of the labour force, but it is highly mechanized and its yields are among the highest in Europe.

Unemployment has remained at a low level, averaging about 1.6 per cent of the working population during the 1960s. It increased slightly during the

Figure 12:1   Analysis of employment by principal sectors

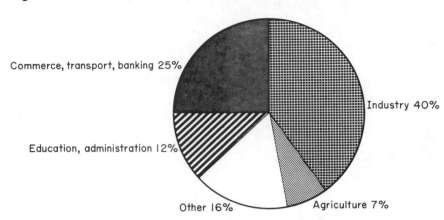

early 1970s.

There is a considerable proportion of immigrants from South Europe, as well as inhabitants of the former Dutch colonies.

The Economy

The GNP (1970) is £12 520 million. The economy relies heavily on foreign trade and Holland has experienced balance of payment problems. Its principal trading partner is West Germany which accounts for over one-third of all imports and exports. The main imported commodities are food and raw materials, while exports consist primarily of agricultural and manu-factured goods.

The growth rate in 1973 is estimated to be 4.3 per cent, compared with only 2 per cent in 1972. The country has experienced a severe cost and price inflation.

Government

The Netherlands is a constitutional monarchy. There is a two-chamber parliament, with an Upper and Lower Chamber, the latter being elected by universal suffrage on proportional representation. There is a multiplicity of political parties, many of which are based on religion.

In recent years, governments have tended to be to the right of centre, but after the 1971 election a coalition was formed between five political parties which was basically left of centre. This government resigned in June 1972 and the subsequent general election produced an inconclusive result. Mr B. W. Biesheuvel, former coalition Prime Minister, headed a caretaker government in Autumn 1973.

Population density in principal regions

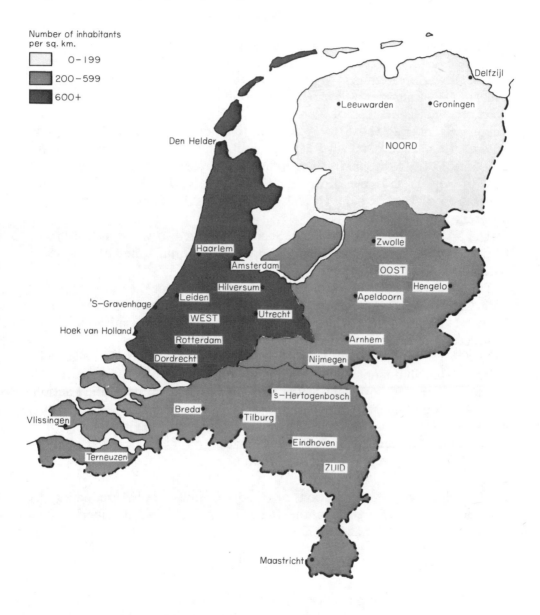

Number of inhabitants
per sq. km.

	0–199
	200–599
	600+

Delfzijl

Leeuwarden   Groningen

NOORD

Den Helder

Haarlem

Zwolle

Amsterdam

OOST

Hilversum

Hengelo

'S-Gravenhage   Leiden

Apeldoorn

WEST   Utrecht

Hoek van Holland

Rotterdam   Arnhem

Dordrecht   Nijmegen

's-Hertogenbosch

Breda   Tilburg

Vlissingen

Eindhoven

Terneuzen   ZUID

Maastricht

Membership

The trade union movement developed later in the Netherlands than in most European countries. This was because the country's industrial growth was relatively slow and because there was originally a ban on free association, both for workers and employers. The General Federation of Dutch Workers (ANWV) was created in 1871. It grouped the national and local unions which were beginning to develop, despite the ban. Shortly afterwards, a new body, the Social-democratic Federation (SDB) was formed and a National Labour Secretariat (NAS) was created to coordinate political and trade union action. Its leaders' advocacy of direct action and revolutionary strikes led some of the more moderate members to leave the NAS, which broke up in 1903. On the initiative of the diamond workers, the present Netherlands Federation of Trade Unions (NVV) was formed in 1905, embracing some 30 different unions.

The NVV was, and has remained, Socialist-oriented. It was opposed by the Christian workers in the movement who, in 1909, formed their own national federation.

This body rejected the theory of class struggle and at the outset included both Catholics and Protestants. But in 1912, Catholic workers were ordered by the Dutch bishops to dissociate themselves from an organization which included Protestants. They formed their own federation.

During the Second World War, all unions were absorbed into a Nazi-type Labour front, but immediately afterwards the leaders began the process of reconstructing the movement in the hope of achieving more unified action. In 1945 a Communist-dominated group, Trade Union Unity Centre (EVC), was set up, but it was dissolved after the Hungarian uprising in 1956.

The Dutch movement has remained divided on ideological and religious lines. There are at present three main centres:

1 The Netherlands Federation of Trade Unions, NVV, predominantly Socialist and affiliated to the ICFTU, with 633 142 members at end 1972 – 650 000 in May 1973.
2 The Netherlands Federation of Catholic Trade Unions (NKV) affiliated to the World Confederation of Labour (Christian) with 398 000 members (July 1972).
3 The Christian National Federation of Trade Unions (CNV), Protestant, and also affiliated to the WCL, with 238 000 members (April 1972).

There is a separate federation for professional and managerial unions.

In all, about 1.5 million workers, out of a total employed population of about 4.2 million, belong to unions. This represents about one-third of the total number of workers.

The growth of the various federations since the early years of this century is shown in the Figure 12:2.

Figure 12:2   Growth of trade union membership

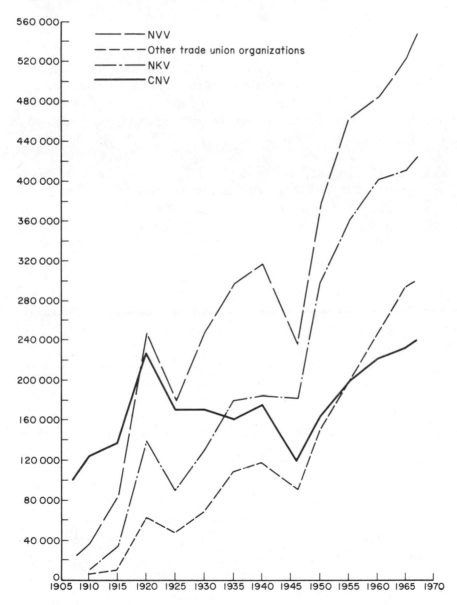

Structure

Each of the federations is organized in groups on an industrial and occupational basis and is associated with the appropriate political party and/or religious denomination.

In recent years, there have been many discussions about the possibility of inter-union cooperation and a loosening of the political ties which impede this. The NVV and the NKV agreed in principle to form a joint federation in 1973, but the CNV have so far been hesitant, for fear of losing their identity. There is already a top-level coordinating body for all three centres. Established during the 1950s, it consists of the presidents and general secretaries, plus an executive committee member from each organization. It meets regularly and establishes a committee to handle specific problems. In 1967, the three centres decided on a common action programme, based on a mutual approach to economic and social problems. They cooperate at plant level.

The NVV (Socialist) organization consists of 15 groups. The three largest unions, each with over 100 000 members, cover general workers, civil servants and building workers. At the lower end of the scale are two small unions catering for soccer trainers and soccer professionals.

Membership of the religious unions is more diffuse. There are 22 groups in the NKV (Catholic) organization, the largest being industrial and engineering (140 000) and the smallest hairdressers and chemists' assistants. The NKV organizes workers in the managerial and supervisory grades.

The Protestant (CNV) membership is spread over 24 groups, the largest being that for government employees (57 000). Most CNV unions are small in size and specialist in character.

There is no system of shop stewards as such, but usually the workers in a plant appoint a delegate to take up their grievances and represent their interests. This development, which started in the metal industry, is spreading rapidly.

All three centres pay a great deal of attention to trade union education and information. Unions are concerned about social and economic policies, as well as about the size of the pay packet.

On the employers' side, the main organization is VNO, which represents most of the large- and medium-sized companies, including foreign-owned firms. There is also a Christian Employers' Federation, but the two organizations are combined in a Council of Employers' Organizations for purposes of bargaining and consultation.

Collective Bargaining and Industrial Relations

Collective bargaining has traditionally been accepted in Dutch law. It was recognized as long ago as 1907 and an Act was passed in 1927, recognizing collective agreements. It is still\ in force, though it was amended and strengthened by special decree in October 1945.

For a period after the Second World War, the government applied a system of centralized and statutory wage control, which it then felt was necessary to the country's economic recovery. It hoped thereby to encourage new investment and stimulate saving by keeping consumption at a low level. No other country in Europe has practised such a rigid control over wages and prices for so long a period. It was accepted by both sides of industry, as a means of ensuring stability and orderly industrial progress at a time of national economic difficulty.

The Minister for Social Affairs, acting through a board (or college) of mediators, consisting of lawyers and economic experts, had the right to lay down wage levels for all industries.

A uniform wage structure was introduced, linking wage rates to a standard method of job evaluation and the level of productivity. Government powers, however, were only used after consultation with the 'Stichting van de Arbeid' or Foundation of Labour, a joint employer-union body. Under the Organization of Industry Act 1950, a tripartite Economic and Social Council was set up which, after discussions with the Foundation of Labour, made recommendations to the board of mediators about the permissible rate of wage increases for the coming year. Once accepted, an increase had to be incorporated in various industrial collective agreements. In practice, local bargaining often led to improvements, particularly in piece-rates and incentive schemes.

The system broke down in the early 1960s, when the industrial climate began to change. Both sides of industry sought to regain their freedom of action. The workers resented the fact that while nearly all postwar controls had been dismantled, those over wages remained; the employers, faced with chronic labour shortages, wanted to retain their workforce and attract skilled labour by offering bigger differentials.

As elsewhere in Europe, it was the metalworkers who set the pace in the dash for freedom. There was a wage 'explosion' in 1963-4 when wages increased by 16 per cent — and it became abundantly clear that central controls could not be maintained. The board of government mediators was disbanded in 1963 and responsibility for collective agreements passed to the Foundation of Labour. This effectively marked the end of the postwar statutory policy.

Since the mid-1960s, industry-wide wage negotiations have been carried on directly between employers and union federations, represented on joint industrial boards. Agreements usually last for 1 year though in some cases for 2-3 years. They often cover a very large number of workers, for example 250 000 building workers are included in a single agreement. They deal not only with wages, holidays and hours, but with such matters as training, redundancy and grievance procedures. There is a legal minimum wage which is now adjusted annually according to fluctuations in the wage index.

Wages in the public sector (apart from railways) are determined by law. For the large concerns, for example Philips and Hoogovens steel, there are company agreements, which may be of longer duration, and often set the pattern for other industrial bargains.

During the 1950s there was a tendency for plant agreements to diminish in importance, but with the increase in the size of firms through mergers and foreign investment, the process is expected to accelerate.

In 1970, the Dutch government, concerned at mounting inflation, introduced a new Wages Act. This allows the Minister of Social Affairs to impose a general freeze in an emergency and to intervene in industrial agreements which he considers against the national interest. In practice, he is chary of using these powers. The unions are violently opposed to the measure.

There is no statutory machinery for conciliation or arbitration and labour disputes are mainly handled in the courts, by judges with specialist knowledge of labour matters. Most agreements lay down a grievance procedure, but this is infrequently used. Settlements are usually arrived at by local and informal contact between unions and management representatives.

Disputes

The Netherlands were virtually strike-free for 15 years after the end of the Second World War. This was due to the continuing cooperation between government, employers and unions and to the universal desire not to disrupt the economy. During the early 1960s an average of only 16 working days per 1000 workers was lost in disputes (see Figure 12:3).

The situtation changed rapidly at the end of the decade, and the traditional phlegm of the Dutch workers was replaced by a wave of militancy. The year 1970 brought a wave of social unrest, largely as a result of rising prices. Trouble was touched off by a dispute in Rotterdam, when the permanently employed port workers found that 'koppelbazen', or contract workers, were being employed at higher wages. The dispute was only settled when employers agreed to pay a lump sum of 400 gulden to each permanent worker. In the meantime thousands of other workers came out on strike and in the end about 2 million employees received the same lump sum to appease them, as a form of cost of living bonus. The government also imposed a general freeze on prices. During 1970, 140 days were lost through strikes per 1000 workers.

Figure 12:3   Industrial disputes in the Netherlands

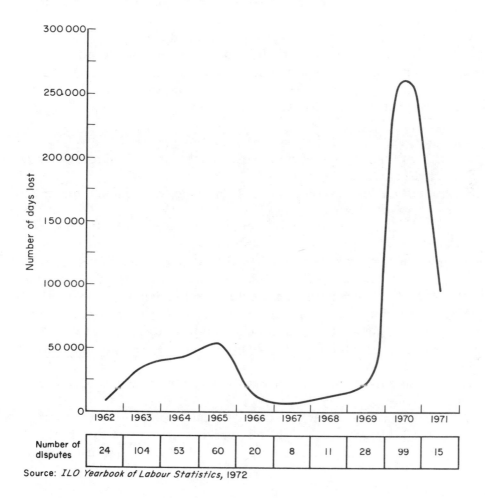

Number of disputes	24	104	53	60	20	8	11	28	99	15

Source: *ILO Yearbook of Labour Statistics,* 1972

The right to strike is not recognized in Dutch law and the unions are pressing for this to be changed. They also want railwaymen, civil servants and other public employees to be allowed to strike.

Employers usually respond to industrial action by seeking a court injunction to order the unions to call off the strike and forbid them to pay strike benefits. If the order is ignored, unions can be fined sums equal to the daily loss of production. The result is often a series of uncontrollable wildcat strikes.

Early in 1973 there was a new outbreak of disputes, which affected some 100 different companies, particularly in the metal and textile industries. Their main object was to get a new system of income distribution incorporated in the 1973 collective agreements, so as to narrow the gap between lower-paid workers and higher-paid salaried employees. The strategy was carefully planned by the Catholic and Socialist unions to hit the more successful concerns. Action was concentrated on the steel works at Hoogovens and this was regarded as a test case for the whole of industry. The metal unions made three demands:

1   Flat rate increases all-round, instead of percentage rises.
2   Salaries of higher-paid white-collar employees to be brought under collective contracts.
3   Compensation for the rise in the cost of living, with a lump sum of 250 gulden for every 1 per cent rise.

A settlement was reached after 4 months of disputes, and long drawn out negotiations in the metal industry. It represents concessions on both sides. Backdated to 1 January 1973, it contains a formula for cost of living compensation on a percentage basis according to the rise in the index.

Other concessions gained by the workers included an all-round wage increase of 1.25 per cent plus 20 gulden a month, the staged reduction of the working week to 40 hours by 1 January 1975, 4 weeks holiday and an increased holiday bonus.

At Hoogovens itself, the 40-hour week was due to come into operation on 1 January 1974.

The March/April 1973 wave of strikes was the biggest since the end of the Second World War. In March, 277.3 working days were lost per 1000 workers and in April, 292.4, compared with only 15.7 in February and 3.2 in May.

The Balance Sheet

During the period of statutory control, the government kept wages and prices in check, but during the 1960s there was a rapid rise, particularly in wages, as Figure 12:4 shows.

Under collective agreements, the working week ranges from 40 to 43½ hours. Relatively little overtime is worked. The Dutch attach great importance to their leisure and family activities.

Figure 12:4 Wage and price index (1947 = 100)

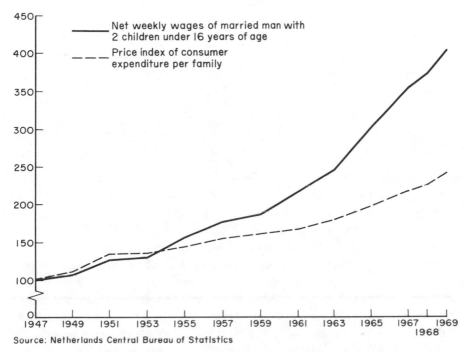

Source: Netherlands Central Bureau of Statistics

The minimum holiday is 3 weeks, sometimes increased to 3½, with 7 public holidays. Sometimes older and long-service workers receive extra days leave.

Dutch workers enjoy a considerable degree of job security. A firm which wants to dismiss a worker has to produce good evidence for its action, which must then be ratified by the local employment office. There is no distinction in the length of notice given to white-collar and manual workers. In the case of collective redundancy the appropriate labour authorities must be informed.

The Netherlands has a comprehensive system of social security on which it actually spends a higher proportion of its GNP than any other EEC country.

The system was coordinated under an Act in 1967. It provides benefits for old age, survivors, sickness, maternity, disablement, industrial injury, unemployment and family allowances, as well as national assistance for people whose incomes fall below a certain level.

Fewer women go out to work than in the UK, about 36 per cent compared with UK's 46 per cent. Equal pay exists in theory but in practice women's earnings are about two-thirds of those of men. The gap has, however, been progressively narrowing.

As in France, there has been a growing tendency towards the adoption of monthly status for manual workers. Monthly payments are made through a bank or the giro system. Another tendency is the gradual abandonment of piece-rate systems and special incentive schemes. Dutch workers are among the most egalitarian in the EEC.

Cooperation

Under the Works Councils Act of 1950, firms with more than 25 workers were obliged to set up works councils — this number was amended to 100 in 1971. There were no sanctions for failure to comply with the 1950 Act. The system is permissive in the case of concerns with 25-100 workers. Councils vary in size according to the number of workers employed. They usually consist of the manager, or his representative, and elected workers' representatives. Worker members are elected from employees who have been with the firm for at least 3 years and all employees of more than one year's standing may vote. Candidates do not need to be, but usually are, trade union members. The manager acts as chairman. There is no separate council for white-collar workers, but where at least 25 young people under 21 are employed, the council must set up a representative youth committee.

The 1950 Act described the Councils' function as being 'to contribute as far as possible to the optimum functioning of the business, while recognizing the independent position of the owners'. In other words, there was to be no infringement of managerial functions. By 1963 about 80 per cent of the Dutch workers were covered by works councils activities.

The revised Act of 1971 required about 4000 enterprises to set up works councils and increased their authority. It confirmed the workers' right to be informed about management decisions and gave the additional right to be consulted before decisions are taken on matters involving personnel policy, holidays, working schedules and conditions, pensions, profit-sharing etc. Works councils deal with matters of safety, health and welfare and are assisted by the Dutch Labour Inspectorate which takes a positive part in promoting these.

Where an enterprise has several factories, central works councils, operating on the same lines as individual councils, are set up. In the event of non-compliance by an employer with the provisions of the Act, individuals or unions may seek the intervention of the Trade Commission, or ultimately resort to the court.

The Netherlands employers' federation is reasonably satisfied with the way works councils have been functioning since the 1971 Act, but some trade unions criticize what they regard as the lack of real participation in economic decision-making. In some cases they resent the tendency for worker members to usurp trade union functions. But there are signs that unions are coming round to support council activities and are training their members to play an effective part in discussions with management on economic and financial matters.

The Structure (of companies) Law of May 1971 deals with the appointment of workers' representatives to the supervisory boards of enterprises. It came into force on 1 July 1971 but was not due to become fully operative until 1 July 1973. The Law applies to all 'corporations', that is, limited companies and private limited companies with paid up capital and reserves of not less than 10 million gulden.

It provides for the cooption of worker members to the supervisory board; these may be nominated by shareholders, the works council or the managing director. A nominee may not be an employee of the enterprise nor an official or employee of a union which negotiates with the firm. Retired or former union officials may be nominated. Both shareholders and works councils have the right to veto any appointment they consider inappropriate with the final say residing in the Economic and Social Council.

The unions are dissatisfied with this procedure. The NVV would prefer the election of workers from their own enterprise, or trade union officials, to supervisory boards and they would like to see 50:50 worker/shareholder representation, with an independent chairman, on the lines of the system in the German coal and steel industry. The Protestant unions have many reservations.

Nationally, there is ample machinery for top-level employer-union consultation on every aspect of industrial relations. The Foundation of Labour, though less important than it was in the days of compulsory wage-fixing, still acts as a forum for joint discussion of labour market problems. The tripartite Economic and Social Council, which consists of 45 members (15 each for government, employers and unions) examines economic trends and advises ministers on all aspects of industrial, labour and social policies, including wages. On this body the Socialist unions have 7 seats, the Catholics 5 and the Protestants 3. Its recommendations carry great weight and are usually accepted by the government. It exercises a strong influence in maintaining industrial stability.

The Dutch system of industrial relations is in a state of transition. There can clearly be no return to the compulsory centralized methods of 1945-63, but equally, there have not yet been signs of a full decentralization. Despite the militancy of some sectors, there is still a general climate of cooperation. The emphasis will inevitably shift increasingly towards plant bargaining and workers' shopfloor representatives will play an increasingly important role. Union leaders at the top are aware that, with this trend and their own preoccupation with national affairs, there is a danger of a gap growing tbetwen themselves and the rank and file. They seek to avoid this by expanding education and training, and by better communications.

13

United Kingdom

Economic Background

The United Kingdom of Great Britain and Northern Ireland has a population of 55½ million, second only in the EEC to that of West Germany. It covers an area of 245 000 square kilometres and has a high population density — 227 inhabitants to the square kilometre. About half the population live in the South and Midlands of England and a third live in seven large conurbations.

Greater London has a population of 7.4 million. Birmingham, in the Midlands, is the country's second largest city with just over 1 million inhabitants. Scotland's two principal cities are Glasgow (897 000) and Edinburgh, the capital, (453 000). Other important cities in England are Liverpool (607 000), Manchester (541 000), Sheffield (520 000), Leeds (495 000), Bristol (425 000), Newcastle (220 000), Southampton (215 000). Belfast, capital of Northern Ireland, has a population of 339 000 and Cardiff, capital of Wales, has 278 000 inhabitants.

Employment

Britain has one of the most highly-developed economic structures in Europe, and the longest established.

The labour force totals 23½ million, of whom 8½ million are engaged in manufacturing industry. Women represent about half the total numbers employed. Less than 3 per cent work in agriculture and over 50 per cent are engaged in the services sector.

The major manufacturing industries are mechanical and electrical engin-

Figure 13:1   Analysis of employment by principal sectors

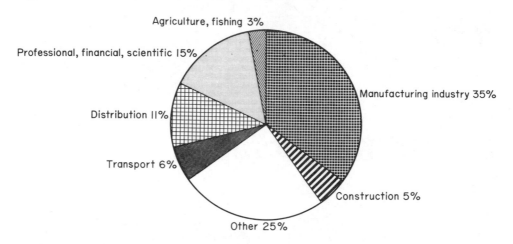

eering, chemicals and petro-chemicals, iron and steel, food, drink and tobacco. Considerable numbers are engaged in transport and the public services, as well as in insurance and banking.

Since the end of the Second World War, there has been a decline in the traditional industries such as coal, shipbuilding and textiles. At the same time there has been a rapid expansion in modern growth industries, for example, computers, office machinery, electronics, and especially cars, TV and a wide range of household durable and consumer goods industries.

In the 20 years after the end of the Second World War, unemployment fluctuated between 1 and 2 per-cent of the working population but after 1967 the rate steadily increased, reaching nearly 1 million, or 4.3 per cent in January 1972. The level dropped sharply in 1973 and in the autumn stood at 2.5 per cent. In the South-east and Midlands, there are shortages of skilled labour in certain sectors. In the old development areas, dominated by the traditional industries, for example Scotland, Northeast, South Wales, unemployment has remained relatively high and persistent efforts have been made to encourage new industrial development in these regions.

There are about 1 million foreign workers, mainly from the Caribbean area and the Asian subcontinent, who came to Britain, before immigration controls were imposed, to work in the areas of greatest labour shortage, for example, transport, public health, hospitals.

The Economy

In the first 12 years of the EEC (1958-70) the GNP of the six members rose by 5½ per cent per annum. In the same period in Britain, the average growth

Population density in principal regions

Number of inhabitants
per sq. km.

☐	0–149
☐	150–199
▨	200–599
■	600 +

Inverness

•Aberdeen

SCOTLAND

•Dundee

Glasgow• •Edinburgh

NORTHERN
IRELAND
Belfast•

•Newcastle
NORTH
•Middlesbrough

NORTH WEST
Blackpool
York Hull
Leeds
Liverpool Manchester
Sheffield YORKSHIRE and
HUMBERSIDE

EAST
MIDLANDS
WEST
MIDLANDS
Norwich

Birmingham EAST
ANGLIA

WALES

Cardiff• London
•Bristol Southend
SOUTH EAST
SOUTH WEST
Southampton Dover
Exeter• Bournemouth
Plymouth Brighton

rate was only about 3 per cent per annum. This was mainly due to recurring balance of payments problems, allied to the vulnerable position of sterling as a world currency. Industry as a whole was slow in adapting itself to change and suffered many competitive disadvantages from having much obsolescent plant and machinery. However, some important restructuring took place, though capital investment lagged behind the level of EEC countries. The GNP was £48 216 million in 1971 and the growth rate was expected to be about 5 per cent in 1973.

The UK is one of the world's five major trading nations and having no natural resources, except coal, is utterly dependent on overseas trade. Its share of world trade has, however, been steadily diminishing and it has suffered from recurrent balance of payments crises. The July 1973 figures indicated that it was running an annual deficit of more than £1000 million, despite record exports.

The direction of British trade has steadily turned away from its traditional Commonwealth partners to Western Europe. Exports to the six original EEC members account for about 25 per cent of the total. The leading products exported are engineering, notably ships, aircraft, electrical machinery and cars, chemicals and a miscellany of manufactured goods. Main imports consist of foodstuffs, raw materials and petroleum.

Nationalized industries include coal, rail transport, civil aviation, steel, electricity and gas, and are administered by public corporations. In some cases, for example civil aviation, there is competition between public and private enterprise; elsewhere, for example British Petroleum Limited, the government holds shares. There has been a strong trend towards amalgamations and regroupings in the private sector, with the emergence of powerful, and in many cases American-owned, concerns.

Government

The United Kingdom is a constitutional monarchy, with a two-chamber parliament — the House of Lords and the House of Commons. The Commons with 630 members elected on universal suffrage holds ultimate legislative power. Northern Ireland is represented in the Commons but has its own parliament (Stormont) which was suspended in 1972.

The two major parties are the Conservative and Labour parties. The Liberal party is weakly represented in parliament, but appeared to be gaining popular support during 1972 and 1973.

The Labour party under Mr Harold Wilson held office from 1964 to 1970, but was defeated in June 1970 by the Conservatives, led by Mr Edward Heath. In that election, the Conservatives won 330 seats, Labour 287 and the Liberals 6.

Membership

The latest available figure for membership of unions affiliated to the TUC (end 1972) is just over 10 million — 10 001 419 (of whom about one-quarter are women) organized in 120 unions. This compared with a total TUC membership of 8 315 332 in 1962. The unions are still a long way from their objective of organizing the mass of British workers. The TUC figure represents less than 50 per cent of the employed population (23.7 million in civil employment) and only one in three women workers belong to trade unions.

Statistics of membership have been compiled since 1892 by the Chief Registrar of Friendly Societies. This list comprises a larger number of unions (over 600) since the basis of compilation is different from that of the TUC, and there are still a number of non-TUC associations. TUC unions however are estimated to account for over 90 per cent of the total number of trade unionists in Britain.

A breakdown of unions by membership at the end of 1971 is shown in Figure 13:2. Aggregate membership was about 10 935 000 members organized in 469 trade unions.

Figure 13:2   Union membership

Number of members	Number of unions	Total membership*	Percentage of Total number of all unions	Total membership of all unions
Under 100	84	4 000	17.9	0.0
100 and under 500	114	27 000	24.3	0.3
500 and under 1 000	52	36 000	11.1	0.3
1 000 and under 2 500	58	95 000	12.4	0.9
2 500 and under 5 000	49	165 000	10.4	1.5
5 000 and under 10 000	31	210 000	6.6	1.9
10 000 and under 15 000	10	119 000	2.1	1.1
15 000 and under 25 000	19	342 000	4.1	3.1
25 000 and under 50 000	15	503 000	3.2	4.6
50 000 and under 100 000	14	1 007 000	3.0	9.2
100 000 and under 250 000	12	1 718 000	2.6	15.7
250 000 and more	11	6 709 000	2.3	61.4
Totals	469	10 935 000	100.0	100.0

*The figures have been rounded to the nearest 1 000 members
Source: *Department of Employment Gazette*, December 1972

Figure 13:3 shows the number of unions and their aggregate membership at the end of years 1961 to 1971 inclusive.

Figure 13:3   Total union membership (1961-71)

Year	Number of unions at end of year	Membership at end of year*			Percentage increase (+) or decrease (−) on membership of previous year
		Males	Females	Total	
		000's	000's	000's	
1961	655	7 911	2 005	9 916	+0.8
1962	636	7 867	2 041	9 909	−0.0
1963	617	7 866	2 089	9 955	+0.5
1964	608	7 944	2 158	10 101	+1.5
1965	594	7 981	2 224	10 205	+1.0
1966	586	7 899	2 238	10 137	−0.7
1967	567	7 795	2 267	10 061	−0.7
1968	545	7 723	2 341	10 064	+0.0
1969	521	7 854	2 483	10 337	+2.7
1970	496	8 323	2 718	11 041	+6.8
1971	469	8 216	2 720	10 935	−1.0

*The figures have been rounded to the nearest 1 000. The sums of the constituent items may not agree with the totals shown.
Source: *Department of Employment Gazette,* December 1972

Union membership has risen steadily, as Figure 13:4 shows. It slumped during the economic depression of the late 1920s and early 1930s, but rose sharply during the Second World War and continued to increase in the 1960s, though at a less steep rate than in 1945-50.

The extent of union membership varies widely between industries. TUC evidence before the Royal Commission on Trade Unions and Employers' Associations showed that in the public sector the proportion was about 75 per cent compared with about 30 per cent in the private sector. Industries with the highest proportion of membership include coal-mining, the railways, national and local government, and among those with the lowest are building, distribution, hotels and catering and miscellaneous services.

Membership is distributed unevenly. At one end of the scale, there are 17 unions each with over 100 000 members, representing two-thirds of the total membership but only 2½ per cent of the total number of unions. At the other end, there are more than 350 unions with memberships of 1000 or less, representing over half the total number of unions, but only 1 per cent of union membership. In textiles there are 24 separate unions.

Figure 13:4   Growth in trade union membership (1915-71)

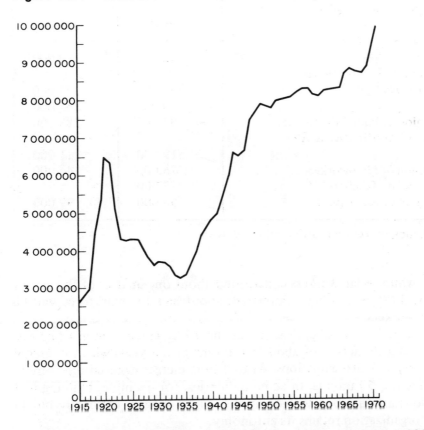

There are some extremely small unions with only about 100 members, organized on a craft or local basis, such as the Sawmakers Protection Society of Sheffield and the Healders and Twisters Trade and Friendly Society of Huddersfield. The tendency is for these small bodies to disappear, as their general secretaries retire or die, and to merge with larger units. Yet their will to survive is often very strong.

The membership of the ten biggest TUC unions is shown in Figure 13:5. It will be noted from the figure that non-manual unions are in the top ten, and that their membership has risen. This growth reflects the national trend.

Figure 13:5   Membership of the ten largest TUC unions (figures are rounded to nearest thousand)

	1972	1968
Transport & General Workers Union	1 643 000	1 476 000
Amalgamated Union of Engineering Workers	1 195 000	1 136 000
General & Municipal Workers Union	842 000	798 000
National and Local Government Officers Association	464 000	373 000
EPTU	420 000	365 000
National Union of Public Employees	397 000	283 000
Union of Shop, Distributive & Allied Workers	319 000	311 000
National Union of Mineworkers	276 000	344 000
National Union of Teachers*	277 000	—
National Union of Railwaymen	194 000	199 000

*National Union of Teachers affiliated in 1970

In 1966, white-collar workers constituted about one-quarter of the labour force but by 1985, it has been estimated, about half the workforce will be white-collar workers.

There were 132 unions represented at the 1972 Trades Union Congress. This represents a reduction of about 50 unions in ten years which is largely due to mergers and amalgamations. At that time merger negotiations were in progress affecting 30 unions. In some industries, for example, building and cotton, unions are grouped in federations, which bargain nationally but in which each organization retains its autonomy.

TUC members are divided into 18 groups as shown in Figure 13:6.

At the end of 1972, the TUC suspended 29 unions for failing to comply with its instructions to deregister under the Industrial Relations Act. Most of the unions concerned were small or medium-sized. Among the better-known organizations involved were: the National Union of Seamen, the Confederation of Health Service Employees, the National Graphical Association (which withdrew from membership) and unions representing bank employees, airline pilots, actors, bakers and professional footballers. The unions were suspended from membership at the 1972 Congress and given until the end of the year to comply with TUC policy. TUC services were withdrawn from unions remaining suspended beyond this date. The suspension of five unions, which deregistered during the year, was lifted. At the 1973 Congress, 20 unions were expelled with a total membership of 370 000 — less than 4 per cent of the total.

Figure 13:6 TUC member groups

Trade group	Number of unions	Membership
Mining and quarrying	2	299 055
Railways	3	297 921
Transport (other than railways)	7	1 742 201
Shipbuilding	2	123 694
Engineering, founding and vehicle building	12	1 523 822
Technical engineering and scientific	5	385 841
Electricity	1	419 646
Iron and steel and minor metal trades	11	148 506
Building, woodworking and furnishing	7	354 278
Printing and paper	7	391 061
Textiles	24	140 521
Clothing, leather and boot and shoe	6	263 592
Glass, ceramics, chemicals, food, drink, tobacco, brushmaking and distribution	10	449 504
Agriculture	1	90 000
Public employees	10	1 401 814
Civil servants	11	667 835
Professional, clerical and entertainment	11	349 674
General workers	2	845 916
Total	132	9 894 881

TUC Statistical Statement 1972

Structure

Because of historical and traditional factors, British unions have developed along very diverse lines and, even in the early 1970s, presented a far from coherent structure. The existing trade union pattern is probably the most complex in the world.

Three main types of union may be identified:

1 *Occupational, including craft.* Craft unions are the oldest and most conservative type. They usually exercise rigid control over their members and over recruitment to the industry and the allocation of jobs. But with the development of modern technology and automation, distinctions of craft and skill have become increasingly blurred and many of the smaller craft unions have lost their separate identity. Examples of craft unions include those covering boilermakers, patternmakers and certain categories of printing workers.

   Many non-manual workers in the professional and clerical field have their own occupational unions, for example, teachers, journalists and bank employees.

2 *General.* These are of comparatively recent growth and emerged at the end of the 19th century as a counter-balance to the exclusive craft unions, in order to cater for the growing numbers of labourers and unskilled workers, who were usually the lowest paid. The two big general workers' unions in Britain are the Transport and General Workers Union (TGWU) and the General and Municipal Workers Union (GMWU). They cut across traditional barriers and follow a horizontal rather than a vertical pattern. There is practically no industry or occupation in which the general workers' unions are not represented. The main and traditional strength of the TGWU lies among dockers and road haulage workers and that of the GMWU among gas workers, but both organize semi-skilled workers, as well as labourers, in engineering, oil and chemicals, and have clerical and administrative workers in their ranks. The TGWU has members in more than 200 industries.

3 *Industrial.* Industrial unionism has never developed in Britain. Indeed, former TUC general secretary George Woodcock said in 1964 that industrial unionism 'is not a runner in this country and is not likely to be in the foreseeable future'. The only example of a fully industrial union is the National Union of Mineworkers, where there is virtually 100 per cent membership. The National Union of Tailors and Garment Workers, the National Union of Agricultural and Allied Workers and the National Union of Boot and Shoe Operatives are examples of industrial organizations, but they represent only a small proportion of the workers in their industries. Railwaymen are organized on an industrial basis but in three separate unions. A variety of unions cater for civil servants and there are two main unions in the Post Office.

Non-manual, or white-collar workers, can be found in all three categories. Many clerical workers are organized in special sections of the big unions, for example TGWU. Others belong to general white-collar organizations, for example the Association of Professional, Executive, Clerical and Computer Staffs (APEX) and the Association of Scientific, Technical and Managerial Staffs (ASTMS). ASTMS has experienced a spectacular rate of growth and its membership reached 250 000 by 1972. As already mentioned, some non-manual workers have their own organizations, for example teachers, civil servants, bank employees.

Periodic attempts have been made to reform union structure, but progress has been slow.

The Royal Commission pointed out that while there are many theoretical advantages in industrial unionism, as practised in West Germany (for example avoidance of demarcation disputes and the harmonization of claims) the practical obstacles are insurmountable. It would mean 'the dismemberment of craft unions and of both the giant general unions and the cutting off of large sections of the membership of the AUEFW, USDAW and the ETU'. Instead, the Commission recommended an acceleration in the process of amalgamation and this has in fact been taking place. The TGWU has absorbed many smaller groups and the Amalgamated Engineering Union and the Amalgamated Union of Foundry Workers combined to form Britain's second largest union the AUEW. Other mergers have included those of the boilermakers, shipwrights and blacksmiths, printing workers and, in the white-collar field, the scientific and managerial workers.

Apart from areas where there are clearly defined limits, such as coal-mining, there is often overlapping and considerable competition for members, particularly in the white-collar field. Some unions, for instance the TGWU and the GMWU, have agreements setting out mutual spheres of interest. Problems of inter-union disputes over recruitment and membership are referred to the TUC Disputes Committee which acts under the so-called 'Bridlington' rules to eliminate conflict. These rules, drawn up in 1939, amount to a code of conduct. They have no force in law. Broadly, they lay down a 'first come, first served' basis, which protects the interests of the union which has already established itself in a particular sphere. Each union is called on not to accept members of another union into membership without an enquiry and not to start negotiations in an establishment where another union organizes the majority of the workers.

The Bridlington procedure operates reasonably from the point of view of minimizing inter-union conflict. About 60-70 disputes are reported to the TUC each year and awards are binding.

The Trades Union Congress

The TUC started on a very small scale and only 34 delegates attended its inaugural conference in Manchester in 1868. It was not until the First World War that it gained national status, and it was still very far from providing collective leadership, or a general staff for the Labour movement. Only under Walter (Lord) Citrine, did it begin gradually to assume some degree of centralized authority and to operate effectively. Even in the 1970s, individual unions are jealous of their autonomy and independence and resist the idea of greater centralization of power within the TUC, which has no formal authority over their activities.

The Trades Union Congress meets annually in the first week of September and is usually attended by about 1000 delegates. One of its main functions is to elect the general council, which acts as the governing body and spokesman for the unions between Congresses. There are 37 members of the general council, plus the elected general secretary. Its members are organized in 19 trade and occupational groups, including one for women, and though nominated by their respective unions they are elected by the whole conference.

In some groups there is no contest but particularly in the non-manual and professional sections there is keen competition for a seat. Once elected, a general councillor can normally (but not automatically) expect to have a seat until retirement.

The general council meets monthly and operates through a series of committees, the members of which are elected each year according to seniority, their special interests and the importance of their union. These committees deal with finance and general purposes, organization and economics, international affairs, education, social insurance, employment policy, nationalized industries, collective bargaining and industrial development. There are also eight industrial committees, dealing with matters of concern to particular groups (steel, building, local government, transport, fuel and power, textiles and clothing, health, hotels and catering). Advisory committees on women, trades councils and non-manual workers hold annual conferences, but do not determine policy.

The general council was established in 1921. Under Citrine, its powers were gradually extended, although he recognized that 'any attempt by the general council to usurp an authority which has not been freely conceded would be fatal to the continuance of the trend which is steadily developing to make the general council a really effective general staff for trade unionism'.

The TUC general council probably reached the peak of its prestige and power during and immediately after the Second World War, when one of its most influential leaders Ernest Bevin was a member of the government.

The general council's functions, as laid down in TUC rules, can be summarized as follows:

1 To transact business between congresses, watch industrial movements and where possible coordinate industrial action.
2 To watch labour legislation and adjust disputes between unions.
3 To promote common action on such questions as hours and wages and to protect trade union principles.
4 To undertake propaganda on behalf of the whole movement and maintain relations with international labour bodies.
5 To take test cases to the House of Lords.
6 To convene a special congress or conference to deal with urgent matters, or to hold conferences of union executives with power to act on behalf of their members.
·7 To prepare a report on its work for each annual congress.

This annual report contains a vast amount of detail about the multifarious activities of the TUC and shows the wide range of subjects with which it is concerned. There is hardly any aspect of society in which trade union interests are not represented.

The report is debated paragraph by paragraph at the annual Congress and resolutions submitted by individual unions are taken as appropriate to the subject matter. Usually about 70-80 resolutions appear on the agenda, but many of these are 'composited', a process which often leads to resolutions of inordinate length and ambiguity.

The general council's authority over member unions is moral, rather than mandatory. Apart from its functions in connection with inter-union disputes, it operates by giving guidance and advice, rather than instructions. Its main sanction against recalcitrant unions is the recommendation that the TUC should expel a union. This was done in the case of the Communist-led Electrical Trades Union, following the successful court action by members of the union against its leadership for election malpractices.

The general council is the main spokesman for the trade union movement *vis-à-vis* the government, the Confederation of British Industry and other bodies. It is represented on such bodies as the National Economic Development Council. It frequently takes a hand in the resolution of industrial disputes, where the national interest is involved.

Centralization of activities has certainly not proceeded as far, or as fast, as some trade union observers would have wished. The TUC is limited in financial and manpower resources — its total headquarters staff consists of about 100 people. Compared with the German and American trade union movements, its resources for research, education, information-gathering and communications are limited. Yet, the modern general council exercises an authority over its affiliated unions which would have been unthinkable in earlier days.

Between the end of the First World War and 1973, the TUC had four general secretaries: Lord Citrine, Sir Vincent Tewson, George Woodcock, Vic Feather. In 1973 Lionel, (Len) Murray was elected general secretary. TUC presidents are elected annually from members of the general council and serve for one year.

The TUC's opposite number on the employers' side is the Confederation of British Industry (CBI). It was formed as the result of a merger between the Federation of British Industry, the British Employers' Confederation and the National Association of British Manufacturers. There are about 1500 separate employers' associations, most of which are affiliated to the CBI. The CBI is industry's principal spokesman *vis-à-vis* the government. It does not exercise bargaining functions, but gives guidance and advice on all labour and industrial matters to its members. Its director-general is Mr Campbell Adamson.

Individual unions

Because of the diverse character and compositon of British trade unions, there are wide differences in their procedures, rules and styles of leadership.

Most union general secretaries are democratically elected by ballot vote of their membership. The numbers voting in such elections vary from about 10 per cent in the AUEW to 60-70 per cent in the NUM.

The general secretary occupies a pivotal position in his organization, though sometimes, as in the AUEW and the NUM, the president (also elected) is a better-known public figure. Union leaders who are also members of the TUC general council are liable to become deeply involved in committee work, whether for the TUC or the government, nationally or internationally, as well as having to carry out their own union responsibilities. They therefore bear a very heavy burden. The present-day union negotiator has to have a grasp of economics and social policies, and to hold his own at boardroom meetings with employers. The days of the cloth cap 'I left school at 14' union leader are passing and many modern officials have been university-educated and gained their union experience at an office desk rather than at the workbench.

But a degree of firsthand experience of industry remains vital if a union leader is to represent his members effectively. Otherwise, there is a danger that a leader who has spent his whole working life at a desk will get out of touch with the rank and file and will fail to understand fully the day-to-day industrial problems which cause frustration and lead to industrial unrest on the shopfloor.

This is where internal communications are vital. Many British unions do less in this respect than those in Germany and Denmark. They lack the resources to promote public relations, whether internally or externally and, with a few notable exceptions, union journals tend to be dull and unattractive. There have been recent improvements, but on the whole trade unions are suspicious of the mass media, although some of their leaders frequently appear on television programmes.

Some unions are well-off and have ample reserves, but many are concerned about lack of financial resources. In 1960, the TUC carried out a survey into trade union finances, which confirmed that most unions were living beyond their means and that income from contributions was not enough to finance the necessary services to members. At that time, the average paid in dues was just over £3 a year, but contributions were progressively increased during the 1960s.

TUC returns in the general council's 1973 report give the information shown in Figure 13:7 on income and expenditure.

Figure 13:7   Union finances

	1956	1961	1966	1969	1970	1971
Membership covered (thousands)	8,549	8,545	8,584	8,753	9,277	8,716
Income per member						
Contributions	£2.40	£3.16	£4.19	£4.37	£4.72	£5.30
Investments	34p	46p	69p	73p	77p	65p
Other sources				13p	14p	13p
Total income	£2.74	£3.62	£4.88	£5.23	£5.63	£6.08
Expenditure per member						
Administration	£1.42	£1.86	£2.62	£3.13	£3.26	£3.85
Benefits						
Dispute	10p	6p	11p	19p	39p	48p
Unemployment	2p	2p	3p	5p	6p	14p
Accident and sickness	15p	20p	40p	44p	42p	38p
Superannuation	27p	32p	32p	31p	30p	31p
Death/Funeral	8p	11p	15p	15p	15p	11p
Total of above expenditure	£2.04	£2.57	£3.63	£4.27	£4.58	£5.27

Figure 13:7 shows that in ten years since 1961, unions' total income nearly doubled, while the cost of administration more than doubled. The value of benefits was more than twice as high in 1971 as in 1961, the biggest increases being in the amount paid out in dispute and unemployment benefits. As well as cash benefits, trade unions provide a variety of essential services to their members, such as legal aid and advice, education and training.

The governing body of a trade union is its elected executive committee or council, which provides the effective leadership between union conferences. These vary in size from the 7 full-time members of the AUEW national committee to the 40-strong executive of the TGWU, the members of which are elected on a 'lay' basis, to represent both geographical regions and occupational groups. The TGWU appoints its full-time officials. In many unions including the AUEW full-time officials are elected.

In all unions, the delegate conference is regarded as the supreme source of authority, which mandates its representatives to vote on certain issues at the TUC and (if affiliated) at the Labour party conference. Most union conferences are held annually, but the TGWU meets every other year, leaving important policy issues to be decided by the executive or by its key Finance and General Purposes Committee.

In practice, only a relatively small proportion of trade unionists participate in policy-making, although the votes cast on their behalf in the TUC are based on a union's entire membership. The vast majority of trade unionists seem content to leave these matters to the minority of active members.

Most TUC unions have a political fund, from which members may contract out. Under the Trades Disputes Act of 1927, contracting-in was substituted for contracting-out, and certain restrictions were placed on unions' political activities. The Act was repealed in 1947. The TUC, as such, has no political affiliations and many of its member unions, in the civil service and professional fields, are non-political. But individual trade unions provide about 90 per cent of the Labour party funds and control four-fifths of the votes at the annual conference.

If they all voted the same way, the unions could swamp the Labour party and impose their decisions. In practice, union votes are usually divided, but, in recent years, the left-wing domination of the big unions has led to a swing to the left in the party.

Shop Stewards

Shop stewards are at the pivotal point of industrial organization and have steadily increased in influence and power. To the ordinary man or woman in the workshop, the shop steward represents the union. Few workers have contact with trade union leaders or with local union officials and union branch meetings, generally organized on a geographical basis, tend to be poorly attended.

Shop stewards are usually elected at the workplace and may represent individual unions or all the workers in a particular shop. Their main function is to be the workers' spokesmen *vis-à-vis* the employers on all questions of working conditions, redundancy, manning and deployment. They negotiate on piece-work rates, hours, local adjustments to a national agreement and many other workplace issues. They deal with union recruitment, collect dues (unless these are deducted from wages), act as a channel of communication and take up workers' grievances. Unions depend very largely on shop stewards for the strength of their organization, both in terms of finance and membership.

In places where there are several unions, joint committees are usually formed, either representing the stewards in the same plant or linking committees from factories in the same ownership or throughout an industry. The TUC, however, is against the formation of national shop steward organizations, or the holding of national conferences of stewards from all industries, as designed 'to usurp the policy-making functions of unions or federations of unions'.

The TUC strongly supports the institution of shop stewards, or workplace representatives. It told the Royal Commission: 'Each year, these union representatives are the instruments for settling thousands of problems quickly and suitably. Most of them work loyally under difficulties with personal sacrifice; it is very few who misuse their office'. In its view, managements should provide stewards with more and better facilities to carry out their union and workplace functions and allow them to attend without loss of pay the training courses run both by the TUC and by individual unions.

Precise figures are hard to come by, but there are probably about 200 000 shop stewards in Britain. The job is often arduous and time-consuming and it is usually the most dedicated trade unionists who get elected. The tiny minority of militant stewards has tended to give the whole system an unfortunate reputation, particularly in the car industry. There is, however, no doubt that direct workshop representation is essential and is in the interests of managements as well as workers.

The Royal Commission was emphatic on this point:

> It is often wide off the mark to describe shop stewards as 'trouble-makers'. Trouble is thrust upon them . . . Shop stewards are rarely agitators pushing workers towards unconstitutional action . . . Quite commonly they are supporters of order exercising a restraining influence on their members in conditions which promote disorder. To quote our survey of 'shop stewards and workshop relations: 'For the most part the steward is viewed by others, and views himself, as an accepted, reasonable and even moderating influence, more of a lubricant than an irritant'.

Collective Bargaining and Industrial Relations

In its evidence before the Royal Commission the TUC stated that of all union objectives, that of 'improved wages and terms of employment stands at the top of the list'. It emphasized that this could only be achieved through voluntary collective bargaining. 'Collective bargaining is the most important trade union method. It is in fact more than a method, it is the central feature of trade unionism'. The TGWU evidence reiterated this point: 'We believe that the primary function of trade unions is to maintain and improve the conditions of their members' working lives by effective collective bargaining'.

Insistence on the voluntary nature of collective bargaining is the cornerstone of trade union policy. It explains the hostility to proposals contained in the Labour government's white paper *In Place of Strife* and to the Conservative Industrial Relations Act, both of which involved the law in the field of industrial relations. It also accounts for the resistance to the pay freezes introduced by both governments. A return to free collective bargaining was a central point in the TUC discussions with the government on prices and incomes in the summer of 1973.

No doubt the TUC would share the views expressed by Sir Winston Churchill in 1951, when the newly-elected Conservative government decided not to re-enact the Trades Disputes Act of 1927 (which placed certain curbs on unions' political activities and substituted contracting-in for contracting-out of the political levy): 'The question may well be left to common sense and the British way of doing things.'

The TUC has always been a pragmatic body and has steered clear of theoretical and ideological considerations which characterize many of the Continental trade unions. It tends to judge each issue on its merits and to face each problem as it arises.

Wages in Britain are fixed by a variety of methods. For workers in the less well-organized industries, such as food and distribution, clothing, laundries, there is a network of wages councils, which fix minimum remuneration and holidays. These councils cover about 3 million workers. They date from an Act of 1945 and replace the trade boards, which were originally created in 1909 to protect workers against 'sweating'. The wages councils are composed of equal numbers of employers' and workers' representatives plus a small number of independent members. There is a separate wages board for agriculture. In some sectors, for example distribution, wages council rates are supplemented by local agreements.

Over the broad field of industry, wages and conditions of employment are determined by voluntary negotiations between employers and trade union leaders. As the Ministry of Labour put it in evidence to the Royal Commission: 'The main feature of the British system of industrial relations is the voluntary machinery which has grown up over a wide area of employment for industry-wide collective bargaining and discussion between employers' associations and trade unions over terms and conditions of employment.' In most industries, bargaining machinery exists at national level, leaving adjustments and interpretation to local agreement and plant bargaining. In some cases there is a degree of sectional bargaining. Thus in the National Health Service, nine different functional councils cover the various groups involved. There is separate negotiating machinery for the railways, the civil service and mining. Generally white-collar workers are dealt with in separate negotiations.

Most industrial agreements specify remuneration for a normal working week and for holidays with pay and usually lay down rates for craftsmen and labourers and juveniles and women. Frequently, as in engineering the nationally agreed rate serves merely as a minimum. Sometimes different rates are agreed for London and the provinces. National agreements often cover such matters as shift working, overtime, apprenticeships, redundancy, sick pay and pensions but such matters may be settled locally. Local agreements usually deal with such questions as piecework rates, bonus payments, allowances and merit money and work arrangements. Issues of discipline, safety, redundancy, health and welfare are normally handled at local level between managements and the workers' representatives.

About 2 million workers have built-in cost of living agreements, adjusting wages according to movements in the retail price index.

Some post-war trends in collective bargaining may be noted:

1   The development of plant bargaining, as distinct from national wage-fixing. In the oil industry, for example, there are company agreements covering every section in distribution, refining and production.
2   The growth of productivity bargaining, in which unions usually agree to abandon certain restrictions or demarcation lines in return for a share of anticipated future profits resulting from increased productivity. Pioneer in this development was the ESSO oil refinery at Fawley. When unemployment rose steeply in the 1970s, productivity bargaining fell out of favour with the unions.
3   The tendency to adopt a fixed period agreement, usually on a 1-3 year basis, with annual pay rises.
4   The expansion of the range of bargaining issues to cover such matters as occupational pensions, sick pay, and work arrangements.

Some collective agreements lay down specific procedures for the settlement of grievances and the avoidance of disputes. Such procedures exist, for instance, in building, engineering, chemicals and the nationalized industries of gas, electricity and coal-mining. There is no compulsory arbitration, but the Department of Employment has a long-established conciliation machinery, and the Secretary of State is empowered to appoint courts or committees of inquiry into particular disputes. These powers were extensively used by successive governments between 1945 and 1970.

The Conservative government, elected in June 1970, established a new pattern with its Industrial Relations Act, designed to bring some reform into the industrial relations system by applying legal sanctions to certain forms of industrial action and providing better protection for the individual worker. The Act established a National Industrial Relations Court. It continued the Commission on Industrial Relations, set up by the Labour government on the recommendation of the Royal Commission on Trade Unions and Employers' Associations; but it converted the CIR into a statutory body and in other ways too departed from the Royal Commission's view that the best way of promoting good relations was through the medium of voluntary collective bargaining.

Under the Act, the Secretary of State for Employment may, if he thinks a strike would be 'gravely injurious to the national economy', ask the National Industrial Relations Court to order a cooling-off period of up to 60 days. If, in addition, the Secretary of State believes that a strike would be 'seriously injurious to the livelihood of a substantial number of workers' then he can ask the Court to order a ballot to determine the wishes of the union members involved.

Because the Act departed from the Royal Commission's emphasis on voluntary methods, the TUC launched a major campaign against it and decided to boycott all its institutions, though it agreed that unions had the right to defend themselves if taken to the NIRC or to industrial tribunals. A key part of the TUC's objection to the Act is its provision on registration. Before 1971, unions registered voluntarily with the Registrar of Friendly Societies. The Industrial Relations Act created a new registration system for trade unions and employers' associations. Under this a union would have to satisfy the Registrar about the content or operation of its rules and its administration. Unions which were registered under the old system were, initially, automatically registered under the new system. The TUC instructed all its affiliated unions to deregister and in fact only 20 affiliated unions with 370 000 members remained on the register. The TUC secured the agreement of the Labour party that one of its first actions, if returned to power, would be to repeal the Act, and later introduce bills dealing with workers' protection and industrial democracy.

Disputes

The number of days lost through disputes rose steadily during the 1960s and first two years of the 1970s. This is shown in Figure 13:8.

The number of working days lost in 1972 was the highest for any year since 1926 the year of the General Strike.

The first six months of 1973 brought a reduction in the incidence of strikes, compared with the same period of 1972.

The industries with the highest number of strikes are coal-mining, engineering, motor car production, building and port transport. Among the reasons for the strike-proneness of car workers, the Royal Commission mentioned the complicated wage structure and unsatisfactory disputes procedure, fluctuations in employment and the failure of the two sides to adapt their machinery and attitudes to new technological conditions. Many similar elements, for example strong group organization, fragmented bargaining and out-moded wage structures, were responsible for the strike records in coal-mining, the docks and shipyards.

Official figures do not distinguish between official and unofficial (wildcat) strikes, some of which are in the nature of lightning stoppages. The TUC general council has always been opposed to any form of political strikes, but sponsored a one-day protest strike on 1 May 1973 against the government's pay and prices policy.

Figure 13:8   Industrial disputes in the UK

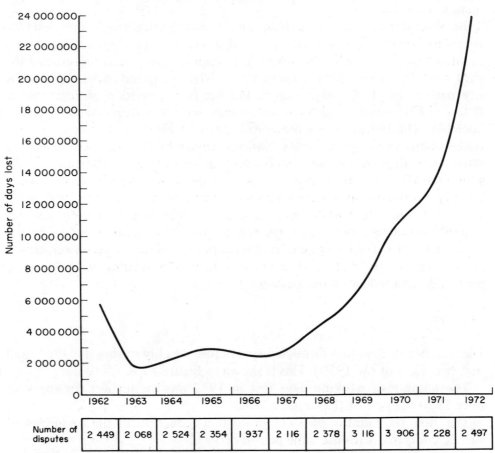

	1962	1963	1964	1965	1966	1967	1968	1969	1970	1971	1972
Number of disputes	2 449	2 068	2 524	2 354	1 937	2 116	2 378	3 116	3 906	2 228	2 497

Source: *ILO Yearbook of Labour Statistics*, 1972

Disputes over wages account for about half the total number of strikes in 1971, followed by questions of employment or discharge (20.2 per cent) and working arrangements, rules and discipline (16.2 per cent).

As well as direct stoppages, workers often resort to such forms of action as go-slow or work-to-rule. Another development is the use of the sit-in or work-in, as a form of protest against threatened works closures or redundancies. The first and most significant of the 'work-ins' was at Upper Clyde Shipyard in July 1971, which lasted until October. Examples of sit-ins include the action against closures in Plessey, Fisher-Bendix, Allis Chalmers and the Thorneycroft factory at Basingstoke. In all cases they have arisen from demands for the 'right to work'.

The Balance Sheet

It is not possible to measure the extent to which trade unions have succeeded in their prime objective of improving wages and conditions of employment. Trade union activities, locally and nationally, cover the whole field of social policy, including housing, health, education and social security, all of which must be taken into account in assessing the standard of living. Individual unions, as well as the TUC, have become increasingly involved in, and consulted about, problems of economic management, production matters and industrial relations. Without industrial and political pressure from the unions, little or no advance would have been possible and, despite the existence of serious pockets of poverty and hardship among lower-paid workers and pensioners, the general material standard of living is high in Britain today. Even so, the country has lagged behind many EEC countries, as the facts given in Chapter 1 show, in its rate of growth and in social provision for its population, as well as in holidays and certain fringe benefits.

As far as real wages are concerned, Figure 13:9 shows the course of earnings, wage rates, prices and wages and salaries per unit of output between 1963 and the end of 1972.

The very steep rise of wage rates during 1970-2, the deterioration in the balance of payments and price increases caused the government to introduce its counter-inflation programme in the autumn of 1972. Stage One of this was a period of freeze, this was followed by Stage Two in February 1973, when the limit of £1 + 4 per cent was laid down for pay increases and prices were to be subject to approval by a Price Commission. Pay came under a special Pay Board.

Weekly wage rates had increased by 13.5 per cent in 1970, 12.4 per cent in 1971 and 13.8 per cent in 1972 (before the standstill) compared with an average of 4.7 a year during the previous 10 years.

During Stage One of the policy, the rise in the rate of weekly wages was slowed down. (The index was 108.0 in November 1972 108.1 in January 1973, 108.6 in February 1973.) Between March and July 1973 after the introduction of relaxations in Stage Two, it rose to 115.4. (This represented an increase of 15.4 per cent over July 1972.)

In the meantime, prices continued to rise, though at a less rapid level. The retail price index in June 1973 was 9 per cent higher than the year before. Food prices, however, rose by more than 16 per cent. Fresh food and housing were excluded from the scope of the Price Commission and, as the TUC stressed, these items bulked large in the budgets of less well-paid working class families.

Figure 13:9   Earnings, wage rates, retail prices, wages and salaries per unit of output

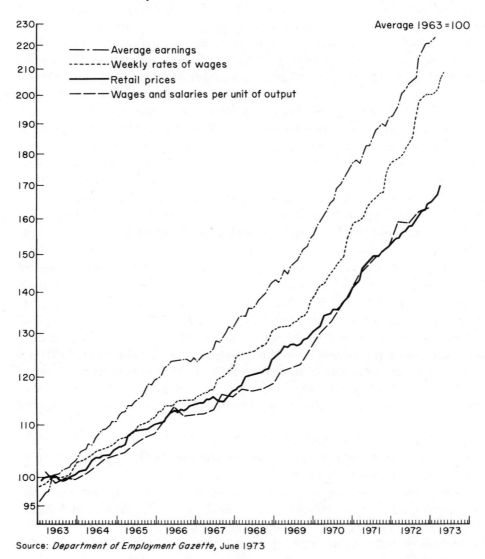

Source: *Department of Employment Gazette*, June 1973

The TUC proposals to the government included stricter enforcement of price controls, food subsidies, a stop on local authority rent increases under the Housing Finance Act 1972, an acceleration in the building programme and control over property development, with higher pensions and a doubling of regional employment premiums. The cost of their proposals was estimated at £800 million. The TUC also wanted a return to free collective bargaining.

Because the government, in its proposals for Stage Three of the counter-inflation programme (announced on 8 October 1973) did not accept the recommendations on, for example, a return to collective bargaining, food subsidies and higher pensions, the TUC declined to cooperate. The general secretary Mr Len Murray said 'It is the end of the line on talks about Phase Three'.

The Confederation of British Industry, however, thought that the government was going too far and that the proposed concessions were more than the economy could stand. Stage Two had represented an increase of 7-8 per cent in earnings. The Stage Three proposals were expected to result in an increase of 10-11 per cent.

The government's proposals allowed for considerable relaxation in the rigid formulae hitherto imposed. They offered two methods for pay increases – a maximum of 7 per cent of the average pay bill, up to a limit of £350 a year for those on £5000 a year and more; or a total of £2.25 a week per employee. Extra payments would be permitted in the case of settlements which removed anomalies, provided for genuine efficiency schemes or compensated for 'unsocial' hours. A built-in safeguard for cost of living increases was included – 40p a week if the retail price index increased by 7 per cent and another 40p for every 1 per cent rise above this level.

The government promised stricter and more extensive control over manufacturers' prices. Among other concessions, it offered a £10 Christmas bonus for pensioners and announced a new Bank Holiday, January 1st.

Cooperation

It would be a mistake to infer that because of the rise in strikes during 1971 and 1972, the general climate of labour relations in Britain was bad. Disputes, as has been shown, tend to be concentrated in certain industries and in many areas of industry and many companies employers and unions cooperate successfully and amicably.

The idea of joint consultation in the UK was first developed at the end of the First World War, when the Whitley Committee advocated the setting up of a network of joint industrial councils throughout industry. Apart from the civil service, the experiment was short-lived, largely as a result of the growing militancy of unions which culminated in the General Strike of 1926 which was followed by economic depression. The practice of consultation was, however, revived during the Second World War, when joint production committees were set up in nearly every works and played a crucial part in stimulating output and cooperation. During the 1950s and 1960s, however, joint consultative committees became less important. They were formed in many of the nationalized industries, as part of the built-in machinery for industrial relations, and in many private companies they continued as works councils, without very much real authority and with negotiations strictly excluded from their functions.

Recently, however, there has been a revival of interest in workers' participation, whether it is called consultation, cooperation, industrial democracy or codetermination. The tendency for the separation of consultative and negotiating functions to be blurred, has been welcomed and encouraged by the TUC, which wants to see more issues become the subject of negotiation, rather than consultation. With the growing importance of shop stewards and plant bargaining, workers have been pressing for an increasing say in all matters affecting their employment and working conditions. In particular, they want the right of access to full information about the company's activities and plans, profits, organization and ownership.

The EEC proposals for worker representation, and the reaction of the various European movements to these, have been described on pages 30-1.

At top level, there is machinery for consultation whether on a bipartite (CBI-TUC) or tripartite (government, CBI, TUC) basis. Both the CBI and the TUC agree in wanting to keep government out of industrial relations. During the late 1960s, the two bodies planned to hold regularly monthly joint meetings to discuss common industrial problems without, as Mr John Davies, then CBI director-general, put it 'the feeling that we were constantly subjected to comment, disagreement and correction by the government'. In the autumn of 1972, the CBI and the TUC set up a joint conciliation and arbitration service and early in 1973, they urged that questions of safety and health at work should be left to an exclusively joint body, without other representatives.

Both the TUC and the CBI are represented on the National Economic Development Council, which is a tripartite body. Individual union and employers' leaders serve on the Economic Development Committees (Little Neddies) set up in various industries. The TUC continues to be consulted by various ministers on different aspects of economic and social policies.

Close relationships with government were established during the Second World War when Ernest Bevin was Minister of Labour and continued during the 1945-50 Labour government and to some extent under the Conservatives during the period when Sir Walter (Lord) Monckton was Minister of Labour.

Relations with the Wilson Labour government after 1966 were soured by its incomes policy and by the proposals to legislate on industrial relations (*In Place of Strife*).

The TUC position *vis-à-vis* the Heath government can only be described as one of suspicion and hostility. This is due to a number of factors, including the Industrial Relations Act, the pay freeze and the rise in prices, and to the government's fiscal and social policies. It is also attributable to the switch to the left within the principal unions and the consequent development of closer cooperation with the Labour opposition.

Sources and Bibliography

Europe — General

European Community (monthly) available from EEC London office, (20 Kensington Palace Gardens, London N8).
European Community Information (monthly), *Financial Times* in association with European Commission.

Commission of the European Communities:

Report on the Development of the Social Situation in the Community in 1972 (February 1973).
Documentation européenne (French and English) series on trade unions 1971-3. (Reports also mentioned in individual country chapters.)
The Enlarged Community in Figures.
The Common Market and the Common Man June 1972).
The New European Social Fund (1973).

ECA Ltd *World Report* (monthly) (9 Orme Court, London W2 4RL)

International Labour Office publications, including:

International Labour Review (monthly), (mentioned in individual country surveys).
Bulletin of Labour Statistics (quarterly).
International Labour Yearbook 1972.

Europa Yearbook 1973, Europa Publications Ltd.
New Europe (monthly) Europa House Publishing Company Ltd.
Europe Left, Labour Committee for Europe.

Among useful guides published in Britain may be mentioned:

Community Europe Today, Broad and Jarrett, Wolff 1972.
W. Farr (ed.), *Daily Telegraph Guide to the Common Market,* Collins, 1973.
Who Does What in the Common Market, Mitchell and Birt, 1972/3.
Margaret Stewart, *Employment Conditions in Europe,* Epping: Gower Economic Publications, 1972.
Labour Relations and Employment Conditions, Coventry and District Employers Association, 1972.
C. E. D. Samson, *Obligations sociales employeurs,* Brussels 1973 (French and English).
Unions in Europe, Kendall and Marx, Centre for Contemporary European Studies, Sussex University, 1971.
R. C. Beever, *Trade Unions and Free Labour Movement in the EEC,* Chatham House/PEP, 1969.
Institute of Personnel Management, *Implications of European Integration for Personnel Management* (IPM Information Report number 6) 1970.
Aspects of Union Policy in Western Europe, Economic and Social Research Institute of the DGB.
European Trade Union Confederation, ducuments relating to foundation conference, February 1973.
'The Unions go multinational', *Financial Times,* 7 February 1973.
ICFTU:
    What it is, how it works, what it does,
    International Trade Secretariats.
    Free Labour World (monthly).
    International Trade Union News (fortnightly).
    ICFTU Economic and Social Bulletin (every 2 months).
    Twenty years, ICFTU.
International Trade Secretariats:
    IMF Bulletin (3 a year).
    European Metalworkers Federation Bulletin.
    News Bulletin (International Union of Food and Allied Workers Associations) (monthly).

Eric Jacobs, *European Trade Unionism,* Croom Helm, 1973.

Workers' Participation

Industrial Relations Review and Report, July 1973:
TUC, *Industrial Democracy* (August 1973).
Industrial Participation, article by Vic Feather summer 1973 and other issues
including winter 1972 on savings trusts.
Some Aspects of Workers Participation, C. Apslund, ICFTU, 1972.
Commission of the European Communities, 'Proposed Statute for the
European Company', *Bulletin of the European Communities,* suppl. 8/70.
Commission of the European Communities, 'Proposal for a Fifth Directive
on the Structure of Sociétés Anonymes', *Bulletin of the European Com-
munities,* suppl.10/72.
EEF News (Engineering Employers Federation), May 1973.

Multinational Companies

The Multinationals, Christopher Tugendhat, Penguin, 1973.
The multinational challenge, ICFTU, 1971.
International companies, report of TUC conference 1970.
International Labour Office, *Multinational Enterprises and Social Policy,*
(Geneva: ILO, 1973).
Articles in *IMF Bulletin* and *News Bulletin* (IUF).
UN report, Multinational corporations in world development, August 1973.
Sunday Times, 7 May 1972.
New Dawn (USDAW journal), July 1973.

Foreign Workers

W. R. Böhning, *The Migration of Workers in the UK and the European
Community,* OUP 1972.
David Stephen, *The EEC and the Migration of British Workers,* Runnymede
Trust, 1971.
New Community (journal of the Community Relations Commission),
October 1971.
'The Slave Workers of Europe', *Sunday Times,* 22 July 1973.
The Times, 30 July and 1 August 1973.
Other publications of the Runnymede Trust, 1 Tudor Street London EC4Y
0AD

Equal Pay

Office of Manpower Economics. *Equal Pay — 1st Report on the Implement-*
ation of the Equal Pay Act 1970, London, HMSO, 1972.
EEC: The employment of women, report 1968. Report on the application of
the principle of equal pay, December 1972.
'Equal pay and you', TUC.
CGT Conference des femmes salariées, May 1973.
'Europe's Watchdog on Equal Pay', *The Times,* 20 August, 1973.

Quality of Work

N. A. B. Wilson, *On the Quality of Working Life,* (Manpower Paper No.7),
London: HMSO, 1973.
A. A. Evans, *Flexibility in Working Life: Opportunities for Individual*
Choice, Paris: OECD, 1973.

Belgium

Business Briefing in Belgium, Brussels, British Chamber of Commerce.
Publications of the Fédération des entreprises de Belgique (employers):
    Rapport annuel.
    La Presence économique belge dans le monde.
    La Belgique dans le monde.
    Bulletin de la fédération.
Roger Blanpain, 'Collective Bargaining in Belgium', *International Labour*
Review, July/August 1971.
EEC: European documentation: the Belgian trade union movement. Organis-
ations syndicales et contrôle ouvrier.
'Trust and Compromise', *The Times,* 9 February 1973.

Denmark

Publications of LO, including:
    The Danish Trade Union Movement.
    Danish labour news.
Publications of the Danish Employers' Confederation including:

The constitution of the Confederation.
Co-worker, co-owner discussion paper.
Brick by brick.
Papers on educational activities and management training.
Texts of DA/LO agreements on:
Cooperation and cooperation committees.
Work study.
Rules for handling labour disputes.
The Main agreement.
Negotiating procedures.
Erik Ohrt, 'Economic Democracy', *Industrial Participation,* Spring 1972.
OECD Economic Surveys Denmark, Paris: OECD, July 1972.
(Article on economic democracy), *Financial Times,* 22 August 1972.
(Interview with Danish Prime Minister), *Free Labour World,* May 1973.
EEC: La fédération des syndicats danois, Documentation européenne.

France

Publications of Bureau des liaisons sociales (5 avenue de la République Paris 11e).
EEC Documentation: Trade union movement in France. La mensualisation en France.
OECD Economic Surveys: France, Paris: OECD, February 1973.
CGT publications, including *La Vie ouvrière* (journal) *Antoinette* (women's journal), *La CGT et les sociétés multinationales,* reports of Congress and joint CGT-CFDT declarations.
J.-J. Oechslin, 'The role of employers organizations,' *International Labour Review,* November 1972.
Y. Delamotte, 'Collective bargaining in France', *International Labour Review,* April 1971.
The Economist, economic survey, December 1972.
Financial Times supplement, 14 May 1973.
The Times supplement, November 1972.

Federal Republic of Germany

Alfred Grosser, *Germany in Our Time,* Praeger, 1971,
The History of the German Labour Movement, Grebing, Wolff 1972.

Publications of the DGB (Trade union):
  Actual aims and problems of German trade unions.
  Areas of Power.
  Basic Programme of the DGB.
  Gemeinwirtschaft.
Publications of the BDA (employers):
  The confederation of German employers associations.
  Expansion of codetermination in the Federal Republic.
  Works Constitution Act, 1972.
Report on Federal Republic of Germany, Barclays Bank Group Economic
Intelligence Unit, May 1973.
Department of Employment, The employment of British workers in
Germany.
EEC Documentation: Trade unions in Germany.
Report, 'Mitbestimmung im Unternehmen', Biedenkopf, Bonn 1970.
H. Reichel, 'Recent trends in collective bargaining'. *International Labour
Review,* December 1971.

Republic of Ireland

Irish TUC:
  Publications, including monthly *Trade Union Information,* annual report
  etc.
ITGWU:
  Publications including *Liberty* (monthly), annual report and history *The
  Planting of the Seed.*
  EEC Documentation: Le movement syndical irlandais.
  Employer/Labour conference, Text of National Agreement 1972.
Official publications:
  The Labour Court, review and reports.
  Information Bulletin.
  Text of Industrial Relations Act 1946 and 1969.
  Journal of Statistics.
Employers (FUE) Industrial relations, Bulletin and annual report.
OECD Economic Surveys: Ireland, Paris: OECD, March 1973.

Italy

OECD Economic Surveys:Italy, Paris: OECD, November 1972.
EEC Documentation: Trade unions in Italy.
G. Giugni, 'Collective bargaining in Italy', *International Labour Review,* October 1971.
Il futura dei sindacati, Sanson, Florence, December 1972.
FIAT, reports and documents on industrial relations.
The Guardian, 24 November 1972.
The Times 29 December 1972 (article on industrial relations).

Netherlands

EEC Documentation: The trade union movement in the Netherlands. Les relations entre les employeurs et les travailleurs.
OECD Economic Surveys: Netherlands, Paris: OECD, April 1970.
W. Albeda, 'Recent trends in collective bargaining', *International Labour Review,* March 1971.
The Netherlands economy in 1973, Central Planning Bureau study.
Social security in the Netherlands, January 1973.
'Going Dutch', *Industrial Society,* June 1973.
The Netherlands, Work and Prosperity, Patthus/Van der Spek 1971.
Articles on strikes in *The Times,* 23 February and 16 March 1973 and *Financial Times,* 15 March 1973.

United Kingdom

TUC, Annual report and various publications including:
    Report on the Industrial Relations Bill, March 1971
    Special Report on Equal Pay, 1970.
    Good Industrial Relations, a Guide, 1971.
    Facilities for Shop Stewards, 1972.
    Labour, Information broadsheet, monthly.
Royal Commission on Trade Unions and Employers' Association:
    Report (Cmnd 3623), HMSO, 1968.

Minutes of Evidence
    2 and 3 (Ministry of Labour), HMSO, 1966.
    24 (Amalgamated Engineering Union), HMSO, 1966.
    30 (Transport and General Workers Union), HMSO, 1966.
    61 (Trades Union Congress), HMSO, 1967.
B. C. Roberts and S. Rothwell, 'Collective bargaining in the UK', *International Labour Review,* December 1972.
Department of Employment and Productivity, *National Minimum Wage: An Inquiry* (Report of an Inter-Departmental Working Party), HMSO, 1969.
Department of Employment Gazette.
Department of employment, *Methods of Payment of Wages* (Report of a Committee of the National Joint Advisory Council), HMSO, 1972.
Industrial Society, White collar union.
A. Buchan, *The Right to Work,* London: Calder and Boyars, 1972. (On Upper Clyde Shipbuilders.)
Commission of Industrial Relations, reports.
Pay Board *Report 2 April - 31 May 1973,* (House of Commons Paper — Session 1972/73 — No. 363) HMSO, 1973.
British Journal of Industrial Relations (monthly).
W. McCarthy, *Future of the Unions,* Fabian Society 1962.
Publications of the Confederation of British Industry.
Central Office of Information, reference pamphlets.

Addresses in Europe and London

EEC

European Economic Community – the Commission (all main divisions) 200 rue de la Loi, 1040 Brussels, 010 32-2 35 00 40/35 80 40

EEC Statistical Office, Centre Louvigny, Boîte postale 130, Luxembourg 010 35-2 288 31

EEC Economic and Social Committee, 3 Bld de l'Empércur, 1010 Brussels 010 32-2 12 39 20

European Coal and Steel Community, 3 Boulevard Joseph II, Luxembourg 010 35-2 288 31

Delegation of the Commission of the EEC to the UK, 20 Kensington Palace Gardens, London W8 4QQ, 01-229 9366

Information Office of the EEC, 20 Kensington Palace Gardens, London W8, 01-727 8090

The UK Permanent Representative at the EEC, 51/52 Avenue des Arts, Brussels 1040, 01 32-2 13 77 80

United Kingdom Government

Department of Trade and Industry, 1 Victoria Street, London SW1H 0ET, 01-222 7877, EEC enquiries ext. 3579 and 2479, EFTA enquiries ext. 2480 and 2479

Department of Employment, 8 St James's Square, London SW1Y 4JR, 01-930 6200

Department of Employment, Overseas division, 32 St James's Square, London SW1Y 4JR, 01-930 6200

Foreign and Commonwealth Office, European Integration Department, Downing Street, London SW1, 01-930 2323

Central Office of Information, Hercules Road, Westminster Bridge Road, London SE1, 01-928 2345

Her Majesty's Stationery Office, Government Bookshop, 49 High Holborn, London WC1V 6HB

British Embassies in EEC countries

Belgium: Britannia House, Rue Joseph II, 28 B-1040, Brussels, 010 32-2 191165/181709/187600, Consulate in Antwerp

Denmark: 38-40 Kastelsvej, DK-2100 Copenhagen Ø Tria 6360

France: 35 rue du Faubourg St Honoré, Paris 8e, 010 33-1 265 27 10/5, 010 33-1 265 06 20/4, Consulates in Bordeaux, Lille, Lyon, Marseille and Strasbourg

Germany: 53 Bonn, Friedrich-Ebert Allee 77, 010 49-2221 234061, Consulates in Berlin, Dusseldorf, Frankfurt, Hamburg, Hanover, Munich, Stuttgart

Ireland: 30 Merrion Square, Dublin 2, 0001-65678/9

Italy: Via XX Settembre 80, 1-00187 Rome, 010 39-6 475551-5, Consulate-

General Milan, Via Fratelli Gabba, 1A, 010 39-2 862488, Consulates in Florence, Genoa, Naples, Palermo, Turin, Venice

Luxembourg: 28 Boulevard Royal, Luxembourg, 010 35-2 298 64/5

Netherlands: Lange Voorhout 10, The Hague, 010 31-70 64 58 00 Consulate-General, Amsterdam, Johannes Vermeerstratt, 7 (commercial section), 010 31-20 73 91 43

London Embassies of EEC countries

Belgium: Belgian Embassy, 103 Eaton Square, London SW1W 9AB, 01-235 5422

Denmark: Royal Danish Embassy, 29 Pont Street, London SW1X 0BQ, 01-584 0102

France: French Embassy, 58 Knightsbridge, London SW1, 01-235 8080

Germany: Embassy of the Federal Republic of Germany, 23 Belgrave Square, London SW1X 8PZ, 01-235 5033

Ireland: Irish Embassy, 17 Grosvenor Place, London, SW1X 7HR, 01-235 2171

Italy: Italian Embassy, 14 Three King's Yard, London W1, 01-629 8200

Luxembourg: Luxembourg Embassy, 27 Wilton Crescent, London SW1X 8SD, 01-235 6961

Netherlands: Royal Netherlands Embassy, 38 Hyde Park Gate, London SW7 5DP, 01-584 5040

International Organizations

International Labour Office, 154 Route de Lausanne, Geneva, Switzerland, 010 41-22 31 24 00/32 62 00
London Office: 40 Piccadilly, London W1, 01-734 6521

Regional offices in France, Germany and Italy

ILO International Centre for advanced technical and vocational training, Corso unita d'Italia 140, 10127 Torino, Italy, 010 39-11 633 733/632 863

Organization for Economic Cooperation and Development (OECD), Chateau de la Muette, 75 - Paris 16e, Publications, 2 rue André-Pascal, 010 33-1 524 82-00

International Confederation of Free Trade Unions (ICFTU), European Trade Union Confederation, Brussels 1000, 37-41 rue Montagne aux herbes potagères, 010 32-2 17 80 85

International Organization of Employers, 98 rue de St Jean, 1201 Geneva, Switzerland, 010 41-22 31 73 50

UNICE (European employers), rue Ravenstein 4, 1000 Brussels, 010 32-2 13 45 62

International Metalworkers Federation (IMF), 54 bis rue des Acacias, 1227 Geneva, Switzerland, 010 41-22 43 61 50

European Metalworkers Federation (EMF), 34-51 rue Montagne aux herbes potagères, Brussels 1000, 010 32-2 17 91 41/2

International Union of Food and Allied Workers Associations (IUF), 15 rue Neckar, 1201 Geneva, Switzerland, 010 41-22 32 43 33

International Transport Workers Federation (ITF), Maritime House, Old Town, Clapham, London SW4 0JR, 01-622 5501-2

Principal Organizations in the Nine EEC countries

Belgium

Employers: Fédération des Entreprises de Belgique, rue Ravenstein 36, 1000 Bruxelles, 010 32-2 11 84 90

Unions: Confédération des Syndicats Chrétiens (CSC), rue de la Loi 135, 1040 Bruxelles, 010 32-2 13 88 20

Fédération générale du travail de Belgique, 42 rue Haute, 1000 Bruxelles, 010 32-2 11 80 67

Other: Centre de recherche et d'Information socio-politiques; rue du Congrès 35, 1000 Bruxelles, 101 32-2 18 32 26

Denmark

Employers: Dansk Arbejdsgiverforening, Vester Voldgade 113, DK 1503, Copenhagen V, 010 45-1 12 33 11

Union: Landsorganisationen i Danmark, 14 Rosenørns Allé, Copenhagan V, 010 45-1 35 55 49

France

Employers: CNPF, 31 avenue Pierre 1er de Serbie, Paris 16e, 010 33-1 553 67 30

Unions: CGT, 213 rue Lafayette, Paris 10e, 010 33-1 208 86 50

CGT-FO, 198 Avenue de Maine, Paris 14e, 010 33-1 783 66 70

CFDT, 26 rue De Montholon, Paris 9e, 010 33-1 878 91 03

Other: Liaisons sociales, 5 avenue de la République, Paris CEDEX 11, 010 33-1 805 30 40

Federal Republic of Germany

Employers: BDA (Bundesvereinigung der Deutschen Arbeitgeberverbände), 5000 Köln, Oberländer Ufer 72, 010 49-221 38 01 72

Union: DGB (Deutscher Gewerkschaftsbund) 4000 Düsseldorf 1, Hans-Böckler-Haus am Kennedydam, Postfach 2601, 010 49-211 43 01 -1

Republic of Ireland

Irish Congress of Trade Unions, Congress Ho., 19 Raglan Road, Ballsbridge, Dublin 4, 0001-680641

Federated Union of Employers, 9 Fitzwilliam Place, Dublin 2, 0001-65126

Italy

Employers: Confindustria (Confederazione Generale dell'Industria Italiana), 00187 Roma, Piazza Venezia 11

Unions: CGIL (Confederazione General Italiana del Lavoro), Roma, Corso d'Italia 25

CISL (Confederazione Italiana Sindacati Lavoratori), Roma, via Po 21

UIL (Unione Italiana del Lavoro), Roma, Via Lucullo 6

Netherlands

Employers: VNO (Verbond van Neederlandsche Ondernemingen) (Federation of Netherlands Industry), The Hague, P.O.B. 2110, Prinses Beatrixlaan 5

Unions: NVV (Nederlands Verbond van Vakverenigingen) (Netherlands Federation of Trade Unions), Amsterdam, P.O.B. 8110, Plein '40-'45 no 1, 010 31-20 13 46 26

NKV (Nederlands Katholiek Vakverbond), Utrecht, Oudenoord 12, 010 31-30 33 33 16

CNV (Christelijk Nationaal Vakverbond in Nederland), (Christian National Federation of Trade Unions in the Netherlands), Utrecht, Maliebaan 8-8a

United Kingdom

Employers: Confederation of British Industry, 21 Tothill Street, London SW1H 9LP, 01-930 6711

Union: Trades Union Congress, Congress House, Great Russell Street, London WC1B 3LS, 01-636 4030

Other: British Institute of Management, Management House, Parker Street, London WC2B 5PT, 01-405 3456

Institute of Personnel Management, 5 Winsley Street, Oxford Circus, London W1N 7AQ, 01-580 3271

Institute of Directors, 10 Belgrave Square, London SW1, 01-235 3601

Industrial Society, Robert Hyde House, 43 Bryanston Square, London W1H 8AH, 01-262 2401

Index

Adamson, Campbell   180
Agricultural Wages Act 1936
    (Ireland)   122
Amalgamated Transport and General
    Workers Union (Ireland)   118, 119
Amalgamated Union of Engineering
    Workers (AUEW) (UK)   177, 182
Analysis of employment *see* Employment
    statistics
Andreotti, Giulio   134
Antoinette   88

Balance sheet of unions progress
    Belgium   61-2
    Denmark   74-5
    France   90-3
    Germany   106 8
    Ireland   124-9
    Italy   139-41
    Luxembourg   150
    Netherlands   162-4
    United Kingdom   189-91
Belgium
    Commissions paritaires *see* Joint
      industrial committees
    Confederation Christian Trade Unions
      (CSC)   54-7, 206
    Federation of Belgian
      Enterprises   58, 206
    Federation of Labour (FGTB)   54-7,
      207

Belgium—*continued*
    Federation of Liberal Unions
      (CGSLB)   54-7
    Government   52
      Chamber of Deputies   52
      Senate   52
    National characteristics of trade
      unions   5
    National Labour Council   58, 63
Benedict, Daniel   36
Bevin, Ernest   179, 192
Biedenkopf Commission 1970   110
Biesheuvel, B. W.   154
Bill for economic democracy
    (Denmark)   75-6
Borschette, Albert   16
Brandt, Willy   10, 100, 103
Bridlington agreement   131, 177
Bundesvereinigung des Deutschen
    Arbeitgeberverbände (BDA)
    (Germany)   104, 105, 207

Catholic Confederation (CIL)
    (Italy)   134
Childers, Erskine   116
Christelijk National Vakverbond in
    Nederland (CNV) *see* Christian
    National Federation of Trade
    Unions
Christian Association of Italian Workers
    (ACLI)   135